NATIONS OF THE WORLD

SOUTH AFRICA

Jen Green

RAINTREE
STECK-VAUGHN
PUBLISHERS

A Harcourt Company

Austin   New York
www.steck-vaughn.com

968
G823x

Steck-Vaughn Company

First published 2001 by Raintree Steck-Vaughn Publishers,
an imprint of Steck-Vaughn Company.
Copyright © 2001 Brown Partworks Limited.

Library of Congress Cataloging-in-Publication Data

Green, Jen.
    South Africa / Jen Green.
       p. cm — (Nations of the World).
    Includes bibliographical references and index.
    Summary: Examines the land, people, and history of South Africa and discusses its current state of affairs and place in the world today.
    ISBN 0-7398-1282-3
    1. South Africa--Juvenile literature. [1. South Africa] I. Title.
II. Nations of the world (Austin, Tex.)

DT1719 .G74 2000
968--dc21

                        00–038233
                        CIP

Printed and bound in the United States
1 2 3 4 5 6 7 8 9 0 BNG 05 04 03 02 01 00

Brown Partworks Limited
Project Editor: Robert Anderson
Designer: Joan Curtis
Cartographers: William Le Bihan and
  Colin Woodman
Picture Researcher: Brenda Clynch
Editorial Assistant: Roland Ellis
Indexer: Kay Ollerenshaw

Raintree Steck-Vaughn
Publishing Director: Walter Kossmann
Art Director: Max Brinkmann

Front cover: thorn tree in an African landscape (background); a Zulu woman making a traditional Zulu drink (bottom left); woven pots (top left)
Title page: South Africa's national flower, the king protea

The acknowledgments on p. 128 form part of this copyright page.

Contents

Foreword

Since ancient times, people have gathered together in communities where they could share and trade resources and strive to build a safe and happy environment. Gradually, as populations grew and societies became more complex, communities expanded to become nations—groups of people who felt sufficiently bound by a common heritage to work together for a shared future.

Land has usually played an important role in defining a nation. People have a natural affection for the landscape in which they grew up. They are proud of its natural beauties—the mountains, rivers, and forests—and of the towns and cities that flourish there. People are proud, too, of their nation's history—the shared struggles and achievements that have shaped the way they live today.

Religion, culture, race, and lifestyle, too, have sometimes played a role in fostering a nation's identity. Often, though, a nation includes people of different races, beliefs, and customs. Many may have come from distant countries.

Nations have rarely been fixed, unchanging things, either territorially or racially. Throughout history, borders have changed, often under the pressure of war, and people have migrated across the globe in search of a new life or because they are fleeing from oppression or disaster. The world's nations are still changing today: Some nations are breaking up and new nations are forming.

South Africa has been the meeting place of many peoples and cultures. In the past, this has resulted in conflict and bloodshed, as various peoples fought for possession of the country's land and resources. For most of South Africa's modern history, a white European minority dominated the black majority, denying them any say in how their country was ruled or how they lived their lives. More recently, however, South Africa has shown how different peoples can work together to forge a single nation. Everyone recognizes that there is still a lot of work to do but remains hopeful for the future of this "rainbow nation."

Introduction

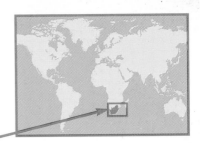

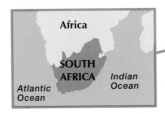

South Africa lies at the southern tip of Africa, surrounded on three sides by the Atlantic and Indian oceans. It is a land of natural beauty and open spaces. Most of the country consists of a high plateau fringed by tall mountains. South Africa has wildlife in abundance and many different kinds of trees and flowers.

Recent years have brought dramatic changes to South Africa, and few countries have been more in the news. Until 1994, the country was ruled by white people of mainly British and Dutch descent, who made up only a small percentage of the population. Black Africans, the majority of the population, had no say in their country's government and could not vote in national elections.

The whites dominated South Africa by means of a system of racial separation called *apartheid*. Many people condemned the system, but it continued in force until the early 1990s. Then, in a few short years, the whole system was swept away and blacks were allowed to vote in a national election for the first time. In 1994, South Africa's first nonracial democratic election took place and a new government was elected, with the black leader Nelson Mandela as president. The event was celebrated around the world as a great leap forward for democracy and freedom.

South Africa's bright hopes for the future were summed up by President Mandela in the following words: "We shall build the society in which...both

Satin flowers carpet the land in the Namaqualand region in northwest South Africa. This area is famous for its glorious displays of wildflowers.

FACT FILE

• South Africa's official name is the Republic of South Africa, or in the Afrikaans language, *Republiek van Suid-Afrika.*

• South Africa has three capitals— Pretoria, Cape Town, and Bloemfontein.

• South Africa's national flower is the king protea, an evergreen shrub.

• South Africa's national animal is the springbok, a kind of antelope. The springbok is included in the country's coat of arms.

• South Africa produces more gold than any other nation. In 1996, the country produced more than 545 tons (494 t) of gold.

black and white will be able to walk tall, without any fear in their hearts...a rainbow nation at peace with itself and the world." Still, South Africa faces many problems, including poverty, many inequalities that are the legacy of apartheid, and a soaring crime rate.

PEOPLES AND LANGUAGES

South Africa's full name is the Republic of South Africa, or *Republiek van Suid-Afrika* in the Afrikaans language. South Africa is a democracy, with an elected parliament and an elected president. The new flag, adopted in 1994, contains six colors and represents all the peoples of South Africa coming together. The South African currency is the rand, written as R.

The "rainbow nation" of South Africa is made up of many different peoples. South Africa's first inhabitants were the San (or Bushmen) and Khoikhoi peoples, but today they form only a tiny fraction of the population. By the 14th century, the Bantu, Nguni, and other black African peoples had settled in the country. Today, three-quarters of all South Africans are black, but the black population is itself made up of many different peoples, including Zulu, Xhosa, Sotho, Tsonga, Ndebele, and Venda.

White people began to settle in South Africa from the 1650s onward. The Dutch were the first to arrive and became known as Afrikaners. They were followed by the British, who formally set up a colony in 1820. Today, white people form nearly 14 percent of the population. People of mixed race, known as coloreds, make up 8

South Africa's colorful national flag was first used on April 27, 1994, when the country held its first free elections for both blacks and whites. The horizontal "Y" shape represents the coming together of South Africa's different groups into a single, harmonious nation.

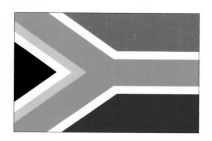

South African bank bills depict aspects of life in the country. The ten-rand bill shows the rhinoceros, which can be seen in national parks and reserves around the country. The 20-rand bill highlights the importance of mining to the South African economy.

POPULATION DENSITY

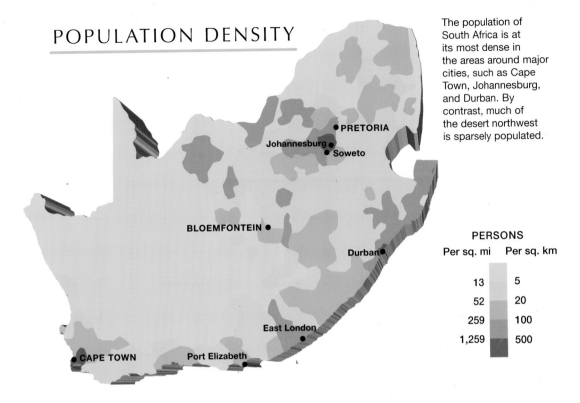

The population of South Africa is at its most dense in the areas around major cities, such as Cape Town, Johannesburg, and Durban. By contrast, much of the desert northwest is sparsely populated.

PERSONS

Per sq. mi	Per sq. km
13	5
52	20
259	100
1,259	500

percent of the population. Some 3 percent are Indians (sometimes called Asians), who came to work in the country during the 19th and 20th centuries.

This mix of peoples means that many different languages are spoken in South Africa. The country has no fewer than 11 official languages, including Zulu, Xhosa, SeSotho, English, and Afrikaans (the language of the Afrikaner people).

The population of South Africa today is about 44 million people. This gives an average population density of 92 people per square mile (36 per sq. km). However, the population is not evenly spread throughout the country. The majority of people live in the east and in the Cape Town area in the far southwest.

South Africa's population increased steeply in the late 20th century.

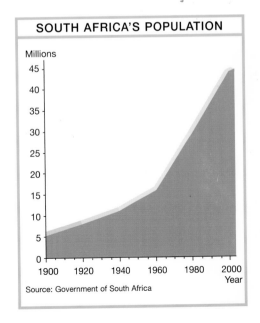

SOUTH AFRICA'S POPULATION

Source: Government of South Africa

9

During apartheid, blacks and coloreds were forced to live in designated areas outside the cities. As a result, the urban population was mainly white. Since 1994, this situation has been changing and South African cities are becoming increasingly racially mixed places.

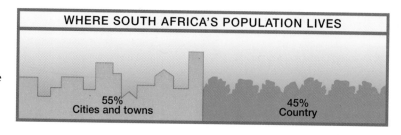

WHERE SOUTH AFRICA'S POPULATION LIVES

55%
Cities and towns

45%
Country

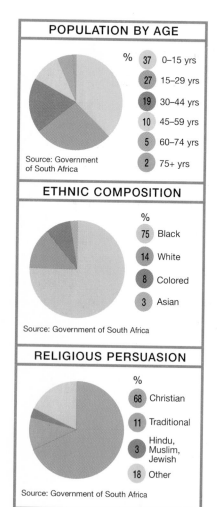

POPULATION BY AGE

%	
37	0–15 yrs
27	15–29 yrs
19	30–44 yrs
10	45–59 yrs
5	60–74 yrs
2	75+ yrs

Source: Government of South Africa

ETHNIC COMPOSITION

%	
75	Black
14	White
8	Colored
3	Asian

Source: Government of South Africa

RELIGIOUS PERSUASION

%	
68	Christian
11	Traditional
3	Hindu, Muslim, Jewish
18	Other

Source: Government of South Africa

Fifty-five percent of all South Africans live in towns and cities. Whites live mostly in urban areas, while a disproportionate number of blacks live in rural areas. As in many countries around the world, there is a trend for people to move away from the countryside to the cities.

South Africa has a young population, with some 37 percent of the people under the age of 15. The population is also growing very quickly. Life expectancy is very different for black and white people. Black men and women in general die considerably younger than their white counterparts. White people can expect to live longer because they have better diets, better health care, and live in cleaner, less polluted areas. In recent years, black life expectancy has worsened despite government reforms.

South Africa has no national church. However, 68 percent of the population is Christian, including 19 percent who belong to black independent churches and 11 percent (mainly Afrikaners) who are members of the Dutch Reformed church. More than 11 percent of the population follow traditional African religions. Other South Africans are Hindus, Muslims, or Jews.

Cape Town and Johannesburg are the largest cities in South Africa. The country is unusual in having three capitals. Cape Town is the legislative (lawmaking) capital, where the government meets. Pretoria is the administrative capital, where important government offices are found. Bloemfontein is the judicial capital, home to the Supreme Court.

Mining lies at the heart of South Africa's economy. South Africa is the most highly industrialized nation in Africa, producing some 40 percent of all Africa's manufactured goods, nearly half of its minerals, and 20 percent of its farm produce. The country contains many valuable minerals, including gold, diamond, copper, and uranium. Mining accounts for almost half of South Africa's exports and 13 percent of the GNP (gross national product). South Africa produces more gold than any other nation in the world.

The National Anthem

From 1957 to 1994, South Africa's official national anthem was *"Die Stem van Suid-Afrika"* ("The Call of South Africa"). The anthem's words were sung in either Afrikaans or English. During the apartheid years, black protesters against apartheid sang a song entitled *"Nkosi Sikelel iAfrika"* ("God Bless Africa"). The song was originally written in Xhosa, but a SeSotho version was published in 1942. In 1994, the new South African government recognized both *"Die Stem van Suid-Afrika"* and *"Nkosi Sikelel iAfrika"* as its national anthems. In 1996, however, shortened versions of the anthems were combined to give South Africa one official national anthem. The language used in the anthem changes throughout the song, representing the diverse nature of the country.

[Xhosa]
God Bless Africa.
May her glory be held up high.
Please hear our prayers.
God bless us, her family.

[SeSotho]
God protect our nation.
Please bring an end to our wars and pain.
Protect us, protect our nation,
Our South Africa—South Africa.

[Afrikaans]
Ringing out from our blue heavens,
from our deep seas breaking round,
Over everlasting mountains,
Where the echoing crags resound,

[English]
Sounds the call to come together,
And united we shall stand.
Let us live and strive for freedom,
In South Africa our land.

Land and Cities

"[The desert of] Namaqualand...tells the truth about the brevity of life, while offering flowers as a symbol of hope and courage."

Author Freeman Paterson

South Africa covers 471,445 square miles (1,221,043 sq. km) of land in the Southern Hemisphere—an area almost twice the size of Texas. North to south the country stretches nearly 1,300 miles (2,000 km), from the Zimbabwean border to Cape Agulhas.

Occupying the southern tip of the African continent, the country is bordered on three sides by sea. Its western shores are washed by the cold Atlantic Ocean, while the southern and eastern coasts face the warmer Indian Ocean. To the north, South Africa shares borders with Botswana, Namibia, and Zimbabwe, while Mozambique and Swaziland lie to the northeast. In the east of the country is the landlocked kingdom of Lesotho.

South Africa is one of the most remote countries in the world. Africa's great capital cities, such as Nairobi and Lagos, are very distant. South America lies some 5,100 miles (8,200 km) away to the west, and Australia 4,700 miles (7,570 km) to the east. North America and Europe both lie some 6,000 miles (9,600 km) away.

South Africa is a land of great beauty. Its landscapes range from red, dusty deserts to lush valleys, and from snow-capped peaks to open grasslands. Along its coastline stretch many sandy beaches and rocky headlands but few sheltered bays. There are many modern cities, including beautiful Cape Town, bustling Johannesburg, and the sunny port and beach resort of Durban.

Table Mountain provides a dramatic backdrop for Cape Town, South Africa's parliamentary capital and one of the world's most beautiful cities.

FACT FILE

● South Africa's most southerly point is Cape Agulhas at 34°52′S. The cape also marks the dividing line between the Indian and Atlantic oceans.

● South Africa is part of southern Africa, which also includes Angola, Botswana, Lesotho, Malawi, Mozambique, Namibia, Swaziland, Zambia, and Zimbabwe.

● South Africa's largest waterfall is Augrabies Falls on the Orange River, where the river drops 480 feet (146 m) in a series of 19 cataracts.

● The country's highest point is Mount Njesuthi at 11,181 feet (3,408 m).

13

THE TERRAIN

Broadly speaking, South Africa's terrain consists of a high inland plateau and narrow coastal lowlands. Part of the plateau and lowlands are separated by a craggy mountain ridge called the Great Escarpment. Both the plateau and lowlands are broken by other features—deserts, mountains, and deep river valleys. Geographers sometimes divide the country into four regions: Plateau, Cape Mountains, Coastal Strip, and Desert (*see* p. 17).

Veld and Mountain

South Africa's high, grassy plateau is called the *veld*—a Dutch word meaning "field." The highest, central part of the plateau is known as the Highveld. To the west the ground slopes down to a region called the Middleveld. In these dry flatlands, water is scarce and the vegetation is mostly scrub. In the northwest, the dusty Kalahari Desert (*see* p. 25) stretches into Botswana and beyond.

In the northeast, the boundary of the Highveld is marked by a rocky ridge called the Witwatersrand, which means "Ridge of White Waters." This area has South Africa's richest gold field and also contains rich veins of uranium and other minerals. To the north of the Witwatersrand lies the Transvaal Basin, an area of savannah—tropical grassland dotted with trees and bushes. East of the Transvaal, the land drops away to a humid region called the Lowveld. It holds the Kruger Park, South Africa's largest national park (*see* p. 34).

South and east of the plateau lies the Great Escarpment, a line of spectacular cliffs and mountains. This escarpment is at its most extraordinary in the east, where it forms a long, jagged mountain range called the Drakensberg (*see* box).

The Drakensberg

The Drakensberg's name means "Dragon's Mountains." In the Zulu language, the range is called uKahlamba, meaning "Barrier of Spears." Both names suggest the mountains' craggy, forbidding appearance. The range runs for more than 155 miles (250 km), stretching through southeast South Africa and across the kingdom of Lesotho. The range holds South Africa's tallest mountains, including many peaks that top 10,000 feet (3,000 m). One peak, aptly named Mont-aux-Sources ("Mountain of Springs"), is the source of no less than eight rivers.

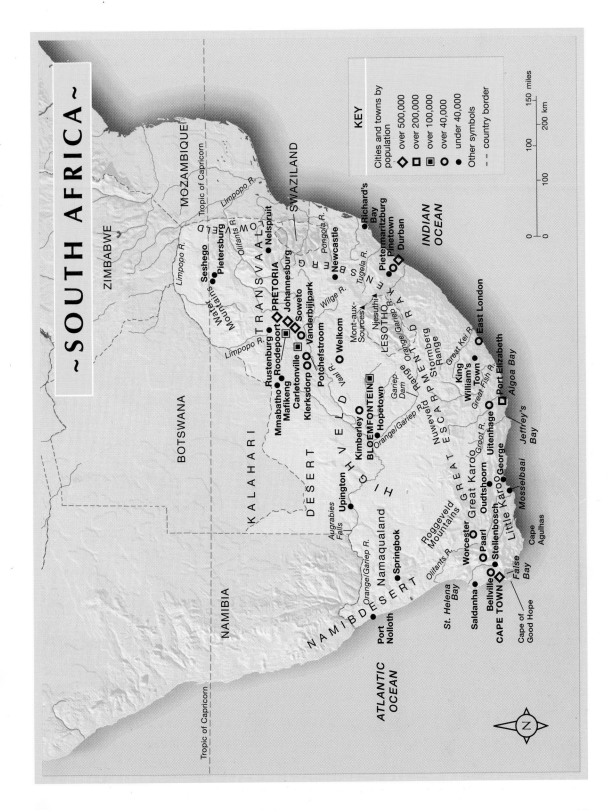

~ SOUTH AFRICA ~

KEY

Cities and towns by population

◇ over 500,000
▱ over 200,000
▣ over 100,000
◯ over 40,000
● under 40,000

Other symbols

-- country border

ZIMBABWE

MOZAMBIQUE

SWAZILAND

Tropic of Capricorn

Limpopo R.

Olifants R.

Limpopo R.

Watersberg Mountains

LOWVELD

Seshego
Pietersburg
Nelspruit

TRANSVAAL

PRETORIA

Johannesburg
Soweto
Roodeport
Vanderbijlpark
Rustenburg
Mmabatho
Mafikeng
Carletonville
Klerksdorp
Potchefstroom

Welkom

Limpopo R.

Vaal R.

Pongola R.

Newcastle

Richard's Bay
Pietermaritzburg
Pinetown
Durban

Tugela R.

INDIAN OCEAN

Wilge R.

Mont-aux-Sources

Njesuthi▲

LESOTHO

HIGHVELD

BOTSWANA

KALAHARI

DESERT

Upington

Kimberley
BLOEMFONTEIN
Hopetown

Orange/Gariep R.

Gariep Dam

Orange/Gariep R.

DRAKENSBERG

Stormberg Range

Great Kei R.

East London

King William's Town
Port Elizabeth

Great Fish R.

Algoa Bay

NAMIBIA

Augrabies Falls

Orange/Gariep R.

Namaqualand

Springbok

NAMIB DESERT

Port Nolloth

St. Helena Bay

Saldanha

Bellville
CAPE TOWN

False Bay

Cape of Good Hope

Olifants R.

Roggeveld Mountains

Worcester
Paarl
Stellenbosch

Little Karoo

GREAT ESCARPMENT

Great Karoo

Oudtshoorn
George

Uitenhage

Nuweveld

Groot R.

Mosselbaai

Cape Agulhas

Jeffrey's Bay

ATLANTIC OCEAN

Tropic of Capricorn

N

150 miles

200 km

100

100

0

15

Coastal Lowlands

The lowlands form a narrow belt along South Africa's western, southern, and eastern coasts. The western strip is narrowest—only about 37 miles (60 km) wide. Here the land is cooled by the cold waters of the Benguela Current, which flows northward from the Antarctic. To the north, the western strip becomes increasingly dry until it merges with the Namib Desert in Namibia.

The winding Tugela River flows down from the Drakensberg mountains on its way to the Indian Ocean. The Tugela is one of eight rivers that have their source on the Mont-aux-Sources. The river was an important natural boundary for local peoples.

South of the Great Escarpment is an area of arid, flat tableland called the Karoo. The Groote Swartberge mountains divide the Karoo into two—the Great Karoo in the north and the Little Karoo in the south, next to the coast. In the far southwest of South Africa, close to Cape Town, are the Cape Mountains—several chains of rugged mountains divided by wide valleys. They include the Cedarberg range, where wind and water have worn the rock into strange shapes.

The eastern coastal strip is wider and is warmed by the Agulhas Current, which flows south from Mozambique. To the west, the land rises quickly to form the plateau lands of South Africa's interior.

SOUTH AFRICA'S LANDFORMS

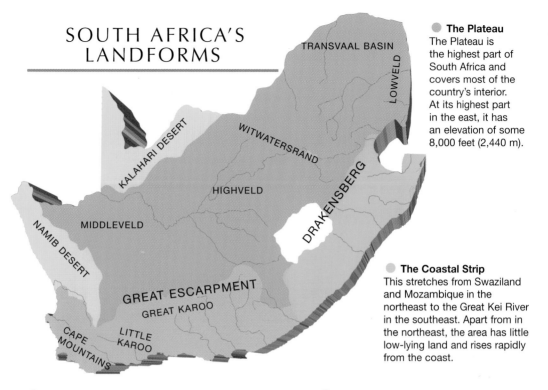

TRANSVAAL BASIN

LOWVELD

KALAHARI DESERT

WITWATERSRAND

DRAKENSBERG

HIGHVELD

MIDDLEVELD

NAMIB DESERT

GREAT ESCARPMENT

GREAT KAROO

CAPE MOUNTAINS

LITTLE KAROO

The Plateau
The Plateau is the highest part of South Africa and covers most of the country's interior. At its highest part in the east, it has an elevation of some 8,000 feet (2,440 m).

The Coastal Strip
This stretches from Swaziland and Mozambique in the northeast to the Great Kei River in the southeast. Apart from in the northeast, the area has little low-lying land and rises rapidly from the coast.

The Namib and Kalahari Deserts
The Namib Desert stretches along South Africa's western coast and is up to 100 miles (160 km) wide. The Kalahari is not all true desert; much of it is covered with low scrub. Few people live in these arid regions, apart from small bands of wandering hunters.

The Cape Mountains
This region of mountain and tableland extends from the Coastal Strip to the Namib Desert. Between the mountain ranges is the Karoo tableland—a vast area of bush and desert and occasional strips of fertile land.

Rivers and Lakes

South Africa is a dry country, with few stretches of open water. The only large lakes are artificial ones created by river dams. The country's longest river is the Orange (or Gariep) River, which rises in the Drakensberg and flows west for about 1,300 miles (2,100 km) to the Atlantic Ocean. At its lower reaches, the river forms South Africa's boundary with Namibia. Its mighty tributary, the Vaal, rises in the Transvaal and flows south for 745 miles (1,200 km) until it joins the Orange.

In the northeast, the Limpopo River forms South Africa's border with both Botswana and Zimbabwe, before reaching the Indian Ocean via Mozambique. The river is sometimes called the Crocodile. Other rivers look impressive on a map but are dry for much of the year.

The Orange River is named not for its muddy waters but for William V of Orange, who was the Dutch monarch in the late 18th century.

PROVINCES OF SOUTH AFRICA

South Africa is divided into nine provinces. They consist of the three Cape provinces that form the western half of the country; Gauteng, North-West, and Northern in the north; and Mpumalanga, Free State, and KwaZulu-Natal in the east. Before 1994, there were only four provinces—Cape Province, Natal, Orange Free State, and the Transvaal, plus the black homelands. In 1994, the post-apartheid government reincorporated the homelands into South Africa and reorganized the country.

PROVINCES OF SOUTH AFRICA

South Africa has nine provinces. They are listed below, together with their capitals, which are marked on the map with dots.

THE PROVINCES	
EASTERN CAPE	NORTHERN
King William's Town	Pietersburg
MPUMALANGA	NORTHERN CAPE
Nelspruit	Kimberley
GAUTENG Johannesburg	NORTH-WEST Mmabatho
KWAZULU-NATAL	FREE STATE
Pietermaritzburg	Bloemfontein
	WESTERN CAPE Cape Town

The Northern Provinces

The provinces of Gauteng, Northern, and North-West are South Africa's mining heartlands and are the source of much of the country's wealth.

Gauteng is South Africa's smallest and most densely populated province. Its name means "place of gold," so it is not surprising that the province is home to the world's richest gold field—the Witwatersrand.

Gauteng's provincial capital is Johannesburg (*see* pp. 40–44). Downtown Jo'burg, as Johannesburg is often known, bristles with gleaming skyscrapers. The city is a major center for business and industry. Southwest of this bustling city lies the sprawling black township of Soweto (*see* pp. 42–43).

Tourists relax beneath the palm trees of a resort in Sun City, North-West Province. Under apartheid, Sun City was part of the black homeland of Bophuthatswana and was free from South Africa's strict antigambling laws.

Only 35 miles (56 km) to the north of Johannesburg is Pretoria, the country's administrative capital (*see* pp. 46–47). Here the pace of life is less hectic. Pretoria contains many historic buildings and a large university. In spring, jacaranda trees bloom in the city streets, producing a cloud of purple flowers.

Much of North-West Province is sweeping prairie, dotted with cattle ranches and fields of corn and sunflowers. Uranium, diamonds, and platinum are mined here. The province's modern capital is Mmabatho. Sun City and Lost City are gambling resorts with a dazzling array of hotels, restaurants, and casinos.

In the far north, bordering Botswana, Zimbabwe, and Mozambique, is Northern Province. The province includes some of the traditional homelands of the Venda, Sotho, and Tswana peoples (*see* p. 51). In the 19th century, white Afrikaners settled the region, and a fierce war broke out between black and white. The Afrikaners knew the area as the Transvaal because it lay "beyond" the Vaal River.

The province has both *veld* and savannah, and in summer it can be blisteringly hot. It is also noted for its rich minerals, including iron, coal, and copper. In the lowlands along the eastern border, the Kruger National Park stretches south into Mpumalanga Province. The provincial capital is Pietersburg.

Pietersburg is also known today by its African name of Polokwane.

The Eastern Provinces

The Eastern Provinces are Mpumalanga, KwaZulu-Natal, and Free State. Mpumalanga once was part of the Transvaal and consists of both Highveld and Lowveld. The west of the province is part of the Highveld. To the east, the Highveld ends suddenly in a steep, tall cliff called the Klein ("Small") Drakensberg, from which there are spectacular views over the Lowveld below. Much of the Lowveld is taken up by the Kruger National Park and by private game reserves. Mpumalanga's capital is Nelspruit. The province's main industries are mining, forestry, and dairy farming.

To the south of Mpumalanga is the small province of KwaZulu-Natal, the homeland of the Zulu people (KwaZulu means "Zulu-land"). The province is known as the "garden province" for its lush, green hills. To the west, the land rises steeply to the Drakensberg. KwaZulu-Natal's prosperity is partly based on coal mining and timber, but mainly on farming. Tropical fruits, such as bananas and pineapples, are grown inland, while plantations of sugar-cane are found along the coast.

On the northeast coast of KwaZulu-Natal is the subtropical city of Durban, South Africa's busiest port and third-largest city (*see* pp. 44–45). Broad, sandy beaches lie north and south of the port. Some 56 miles (90 km) to the northwest is Pietermaritzburg, the province's capital.

West of KwaZulu-Natal lie the mountainous kingdom of Lesotho (*see* p. 22) and the landlocked province of Free State. The province was an independent republic for much of the 19th century. Its capital, Bloemfontein, is also South Africa's judi-

The Blyde River Canyon

One of South Africa's most famous natural sights is the Blyde River Canyon in Mpumalanga Province. As the Blyde River carved its way down from the Highveld to the Lowveld, it formed a deep, 20-mile-long (30 km) canyon. The canyon features spectacular rock formations, such as three huge hutlike rock pillars known as the Three Rondavels and Bourke's Luck Potholes, which are deep, cylindrical holes formed by whirlpools in the river. The canyon is most famous, however, for its beautiful views. The best-known viewpoints are the Wonder View and God's Window.

cial capital. The city was founded on the site of a natural spring—its name means "Fountain of the Flowers." Much of the Free State consists of rolling prairies with huge cornfields and cattle ranches. Farther south, dams have been built on the Orange and Caledon rivers to form a large lake at Gariep Dam.

From the God's Window viewpoint, Mpumalanga Province, there are beautiful views over the Blyde River Canyon.

The Cape Provinces

The Cape Provinces are the Eastern, Western, and Northern Cape provinces. They contain South Africa's most spectacular coastal scenery as well as rugged mountains, lush valleys, and dry plains.

The unspoiled, rocky shoreline of the Eastern Cape stretches southward from KwaZulu-Natal and is known as the Wild Coast. Beyond the Wild Coast are two of South Africa's most important ports. East London (*Oos-Londen* in Afrikaans) was once an important military post, but today it is a bustling port and beach resort. Port Elizabeth is a thriving industrial center best-known for automobile assembly.

Inland lie a series of mountain ranges and the flatlands of the Little Karoo, where grapes and wheat are grown and ostriches are reared. The town of

The word *karoo* derives from the Khoikhoi word for "land of thirst."

Lesotho

Lesotho is a rugged, mountainous kingdom that is completely landlocked by South Africa. It has a population of around two million people, living in an area about half the size of West Virginia. Most of Lesotho lies more than 5,000 feet (1,500 m) above sea level, and the climate is mild and moist for most of the year.

Before 1800, Lesotho was inhabited by an African people called the Sotho. During the tribal wars of the early 19th century, a Sotho chief named Moshoeshoe (pronounced "moshesh") built a stronghold on a mountain called Thaba-Bosiu. He offered protection to refugees in return for their help, and by 1840, his people numbered around 40,000. Moshoeshoe united his followers into the Basuto (Basotho) nation.

Having survived the tribal wars, the Basuto faced a new threat from land-hungry Dutch settlers, or Boers. After attempts at peaceful settlements failed, the British government took control of the country, and in 1884, it became a British protectorate, under the name Basutoland. When the Union of South Africa was created in 1910, Basutoland's protectorate status meant that it was excluded from the union and remained separate. This situation lasted until 1960, when the newly elected Basutoland Congress Party (BCP) demanded independence from Britain. This came into effect in 1966, and the protectorate of Basutoland became the independent kingdom of Lesotho.

Lesotho's recent history has been no less troubled than its past. There have been numerous uprisings since the 1980s. In 1998, a dispute over election results led to violence breaking out in the capital, Maseru, and an uprising by part of the army. Neighboring South Africa and Botswana intervened and restored peace.

Lesotho is one of the world's poorest countries, and its economy relies on residents who work in South Africa. Farming is also important, but soil erosion means farmland is becoming scarce. Today, Lesotho is a constitutional monarchy. The present head of state is King Letsie III, but the government runs the country.

Oudtshoorn is the center of the ostrich-farming area. The town grew very wealthy during the late 19th and early 20th centuries, when ostrich plumes were in great demand for ladies' hats and for feather scarves called *boas*.

Along the coastline in Western Cape Province is Cape Agulhas, the most southerly point in Africa and the meeting place of the Atlantic and Indian oceans. Beyond Cape Agulhas, the coast veers northwest until it reaches Cape Town and the headland of the Cape Peninsula. The famous Cape of Good Hope was an important landmark for sailors in the early years of navigation. The 16th-century English explorer Sir Francis Drake called it "the fairest Cape in all the circumference of the Earth." The region is now a nature reserve famous for its variety of wildflowers.

Cape Town is South Africa's largest and oldest city (*see* pp. 36–39 and 54–57). It nestles in the shadow of the flat-topped Table Mountain. Northeast of the city lies a land of sweeping mountains and fertile valleys—

The Garden Route

The stretch of coastline between Mosselbaai and Jeffrey's Bay on the Western Cape is called the Garden Route. Much of this 135-mile (217-km) route is overshadowed by a craggy range called the Outeniqua Mountains. The Garden Route crisscrosses over high passes and plunges into steep, wooded ravines, past sweeping bays, clear lakes, and several national parks. Oil has recently been discovered off-shore at Mosselbaai, which has transformed the port into a boomtown.

The flatlands of the Karoo are sandwiched between the Cape Mountains and the Great Escarpment. The Karoo sprawls across three provinces— Western, Eastern, and Northern Cape.

The beautiful mountainside Camps Bay, a suburb of Cape Town, is famous for the spectacular "Twelve Apostles." This rock formation runs south from Table Mountain into the sea.

the Cape Winelands, South Africa's foremost wine-growing region. The historic wineland towns of Stellenbosch and Paarl hold many fine buildings dating from the 17th and 18th centuries, built in an ornate style called Cape Dutch (*see* p. 102–103).

The Northern Cape is South Africa's largest and least-populated province. On the western coast, the climate is harsh and dry, but the region contains many rare plants and animals. Inland, the area known as Namaqualand, centered on the town of Springbok, is bleak and barren for much of the year but is carpeted with wildflowers in spring (*see* p. 6). The area was once home to Khoikhoi herders and San hunters, who have left behind their rock paintings (*see* pp. 50–51 and p. 99).

In the far north of Northern Cape is the Kalahari Desert (*see* box opposite). The Kalahari Gemsbok Park straddles the border with Botswana. This remote national park is home to many dryland animals, including antelopes, cheetahs, lions, and leopards.

The Big Hole is the largest hole in the world dug by manual labor and is a national monument. It is 787 feet (240 m) deep.

To the far east is Kimberley, the provincial capital and the heart of South Africa's diamond-mining region. Diamonds were first found here in 1871. The diamond field is the site of the Big Hole, from which three tons of diamonds have been removed (*see* p. 86).

The Kalahari Desert

The Kalahari Desert stretches across much of Botswana as well as parts of Namibia and South Africa. Altogether, this region of desert and dry plateau covers more than 100,000 square miles (259,000 sq. km), an area twice the size of Oregon. Today, it is one of Africa's greatest wildlife havens—home to such animals as antelopes, meerkats, lions, and hyenas as well as to many species of reptiles and birds.

Much of the Kalahari is covered by dry red sand. In summer, the temperature rises to 85°F (30°C), but on winter nights the temperature plummets and frosts occur. Parts of the desert receive more than 10 inches (25 cm) of rain, and some scientists claim that this means it is not a true desert. However, the environment is very harsh, and survival in the desert requires an exceptional ability to adapt. The San were the first known human inhabitants of the Kalahari, and their survival skills have become legendary. Today, only a few members of the tribe follow the traditional way of life and many now live in permanent settlements and depend on welfare.

Mineral companies are beginning to exploit the Kalahari's rich natural resources. One of the world's largest diamond mines is located at Orapa in Botswana. There have also been discoveries of nickel, coal, and copper.

CLIMATE

There are really only three seasons in South Africa—spring, summer, and winter. There is no fall of the kind known in North America and Europe. Since South Africa lies in the Southern Hemisphere, it experiences the seasons at opposite times of year to countries in the Northern Hemisphere, such as the United States. Midsummer falls at Christmastime and in January. This is the main vacation season, when schools close and many people take a break.

Sunshine and Drought

South Africa is generally warm and sunny. Different parts of the country, however, experience different climate patterns, depending on their altitude (height above sea level), prevailing winds (the winds that occur most frequently in a place), and the influence of warm or cold sea currents.

Cape Town and the far southwest have a Mediterranean climate, with warm summers and mild winters. Most of the rain falls here in the winter season (May to August). Durban and KwaZulu-Natal, by contrast, have a subtropical climate; summers can be uncomfortably hot and humid; winters are dry and sunny.

Up on the Highveld, the climate is cooler because of the altitude. In summer, it is hot during the day but cool at night. Most of the rain falls in summer. Winter days are dry and warm, but nights are cold. High in the mountains, temperatures often fall below freezing at night.

Lack of rainfall is a problem in many parts of South Africa. Two-thirds of the country receive

Although Johannesburg is not very far south of the Tropic of Capricorn, its high altitude moderates its climate. It is 930 miles (1,500 km) north of Cape Town, but its average temperatures are only some 2°F (1°C) higher.

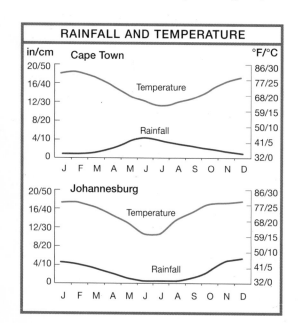

A long period without rain dries a pool in the Kalahari Desert. More than 20 percent of South Africa is arid, receiving less than 8 inches (200 mm) of rain a year. Water shortages are frequent throughout the country, threatening farmers' crops and water-dependent industries.

less than 20 inches (50 cm) of rain each year. Rainfall is often patchy and unpredictable, and drought is common. The rain that does fall comes in sudden thunderstorms in summer. In the heat, much of the precious water evaporates before it has time to sink into the soil. In times of drought, the vegetation dies and the parched earth cracks. Animals die, and some people go hungry.

Rainfall is not evenly distributed throughout South Africa. The western half of the country gets much less rain than the east. This is because the Benguela Current, which flows from the Antarctic, brings cold air that rarely turns to rain. Southern and eastern coasts, by contrast, are wetter because the Agulhas Current brings warm, rain-bearing winds from the Indian Ocean. Most people choose to live and farm in the wetter parts of the country. A map showing where people live looks similar to a map showing where rainfall levels are greatest.

Apart from drought, South Africa also faces other weather hazards. Spectacular electric storms sometimes strike the Highveld. Tornadoes also form inland, with winds of up to 125 mph (200 kph), and can cause great destruction. Along the east coast, cyclones (tropical storms) blow in from the Indian Ocean, battering coastal cities, such as Durban.

Experts estimate that drought causes about 20 percent of the world's disaster-related deaths.

The Cape has the highest concentration of plant species in the world, with some 3,370 species per square mile (1,300 species per sq. km).

WILDLIFE

South Africa's varied landscape is rich in plants and animals. In total, the country is home to some 24,000 plant species—almost one-tenth of the world's flowering plants. Familiar flowers such as geraniums, freesias, and gladioli, which bloom in gardens all over Europe and North America, originally came from South Africa. In terms of animals, the country has been called "the greatest wildlife show on earth." Only the rain forests of the Amazon and Indonesia hold more species.

A Kingdom of Flowers

The coastal region around Cape Town in the Western Cape is one of the world's richest plant habitats. It forms one of the world's six floral kingdoms (*see* box). Other kingdoms, by contrast, stretch over several continents. The Cape is made up of *fynbos* (Dutch for "fine bush"), a heathland vegetation made up of flowering plants such as ericas (heathers) and evergreen shrubs called proteas. The proteas include the king protea, South Africa's national plant. Other flowers in the Cape include a flame-red orchid called the Pride of Table Mountain.

The Floral Kingdoms

Plant geographers divide the world into six areas, or "kingdoms," based on the type of plant life found there. Many of these areas stretch across several continents. The kingdoms are similar to the regions used by animal geographers for animal life. The exception is the identification of the Cape region in South Africa as a distinct kingdom due to its unique flora. The region has more than 8,000 different species of plant, of which 5,000 are found nowhere else.

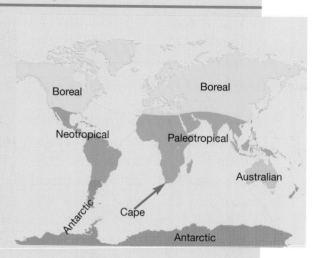

In contrast to the southwest, Northern Cape Province has very little rainfall so that many of the plants that grow here have special ways of collecting and storing water. Some have long roots that stretch far underground to tap water sources. Others, called succulents, store water in their fleshy stems or leaves.

In the barren Namib Desert, the climate is so harsh that only a few plants flourish. However, in Namaqualand the soil contains seeds that grow and sprout pink, yellow, or orange flowers after a rain shower. The desert is also home to a large, strange-looking plant called a *welwitschia*. The plant's long, straggly leaves can gather moisture from dews and fogs, and welwitschias are known to live for centuries.

Savannah, *Veld*, and Woodland

The vast region stretching eastward from the Kalahari to the Transvaal is savannah. A blanket of waving grasses covers the ground, with a scattering of trees and shrubs. Trees of the savannah include the bizarre baobab, which stores water in its swollen trunk. In the far east grow patches of savannah forest, known as *bushveld*. In the central region, much of the great plateau is rolling *veld*. Tall plumes of feather grass and ostrich grass wave above the pale or reddish grass cover, but there are few trees.

South Africa has few forests outside the lowlands bordering the southern and eastern coasts and the well-watered ravines in the mountains. On the east coast of Kwa-Zulu-Natal, there are regions of yellow-wood and ironwood trees, giant tree ferns, and evergreen forests.

The king protea is the national flower of South Africa. The artichoke-like appearance of the flower heads gives the king protea its scientific name— Protea cynaroides ("cynaroides" means "like the artichoke"). The king protea can be found in a variety of colors, but the pink-colored flower is considered to be the most beautiful.

Wildebeests, or gnus, can be found on grassy plains throughout Southern Africa. Their Afrikaans name means "wild ox," although they are in fact a kind of antelope. Both male and female wildebeests have shaggy manes and beards and big curved horns. Here a herd of wildebeests migrates southward in search of fresh grasslands to graze.

The smallest antelope is the duiker, which is just 15 inches (40 cm) tall at the shoulder. The largest is the eland, which is 6 feet (1.7 m) tall.

Animals of the Savannah

Every year, thousands of people come to South Africa to see the varied birds and beasts of the savannah, *veld*, and deserts or to spot marine wildlife in the coastal waters. Each different landscape in South Africa has its own unique wildlife.

South Africa is home to 230 species of land mammals. Probably the best known are the large beasts of the savannah, including lions, giraffes, elephants, rhinoceroses, and cheetahs. The cheetah is the world's swiftest animal—it can race along at speeds of up to 75 miles per hour (120 kph). The giraffe is the tallest animal in the world—a large male stands 17 feet (5 m) tall from his hooves to the tips of his horns. Large herds of grazing animals, such as antelope and zebra, also roam the plains. South Africa's 30 species of antelope include the wildebeest, gemsbok, and the graceful springbok (*see* p. 32). Hippopotamuses are large mammals of the wetlands. Primates include baboons, vervet monkeys, and bush-babies.

Birds, Reptiles, and Fish

South Africa has 900 different species of birds, of which more than 100 are found nowhere else in the world. Some of the country's birds include the flightless ostrich—the world's largest and fastest-moving bird—large-beaked hornbills, crested hoopoes, blue korhaans, secretary birds, and colorful bee-eaters.

Jackass penguins dive for fish in the seas off the Western Cape. Birds of prey include fish eagles and crowned eagles. Waterbirds include pelicans and the blue crane, which is South Africa's national bird.

The country's 230 reptile species include crocodiles, many kinds of tortoises, and 160 different snakes. Dangerous snakes range from the deadly Cape cobra and the black mamba to the African python. The latter is the world's largest snake, growing up to 23 feet (7 m) in length. Lizards include the rock monitor, a giant species that can grow up to 3 feet (1 m) long.

There is also huge variety in South Africa's marine (sea) life. Marine mammals range from giant sperm and killer whales to seals and bottle-nosed dolphins. Fish include sharks and the coelacanth—a rare, primitive fish with stumpy fins that was thought to be extinct until a living specimen was caught in 1938.

A blue korhaan watches over its nest. The korhaan belongs to the bustard family and is famous for its keen eyesight and timid nature.

The Springbok: South Africa's National Animal

The springbok, or springbuck, is the national animal and sporting emblem of South Africa. It is a type of gazelle that is found across southern Africa.

The springbok's name comes from two Afrikaans words meaning "jump" and "goat." It gets its name because when this graceful animal becomes alarmed or excited, it leaps repeatedly into the air in order to distract its predators before galloping away. Its powerful limbs and light frame allow it to leap as high as 11.5 feet (3.5 m).

The slender springbok stands around 2.5 feet (75 cm) high and weighs about 90 pounds (40 kg). Apart from a white face and underside, it is brownish red in color. Both sexes have long, curved horns.

In South Africa, springboks have adapted to dry, barren areas and open grass plains and are found in the Free State, North-West Province, and along the west coast. In the winter months, they roam in small herds. During the summer, however, they crowd together in larger groups. Springboks eat both grass and leaves. They can go without water for long periods because they use the moisture from succulent leaves.

In the past, large numbers of springboks were killed by Dutch settlers because the animals trampled crops while seeking food and water. As a result, today large herds are rarely seen outside the nature reserves and game parks of South Africa.

South Africa's National Parks and Wilderness Areas

Kruger National Park (game reserve)

Pilanesberg National Park (mountain grassland and game reserve)

Kalahari-Gemsbok National Park (desert game reserve)

● Pretoria

Johannesburg ●

Itala Game Reserve

Richtersveld National Park

Augrabies Falls National Park (Orange River landscape)

Golden Gate National Park (mountain landscape)

Mkuzi Game Reserve

Greater St. Lucia (coastal wetland)

Durban ●

Hluhluwe-Umfolozi Game Reserve (famous for its rhinoceroses)

Karoo National Park (desert and mountainous landscape)

Mountain Zebra National Park (haven for the endangered Cape mountain zebra)

Natal Drakensberg (mountain landscape)

West Coast National Park (Coastal and wetland wilderness)

Wilderness National Park (coastal and fynbos landscape)

Cape Town ●

Tsitsikamma National Park (forest and coastal landscape)

Addo Elephant National Park (haven for endangered species)

Limpopo R.

Olifants R.

Orange/Gariep R.

Conserving South Africa's Wildlife

South Africa's wildlife faces many dangers. As in many countries, the biggest enemy is humankind. Mining, farming, and the spread of cities and factories mean that animals have ever smaller territories in which to feed and roam. Soil erosion, pollution, and the spread of deserts are also threats. In the past, hunters and poachers killed big cats, such as leopards and cheetahs, for their beautiful fur, and shot elephants and rhinoceroses for their tusks and horns. Today, South African law protects all these creatures.

Before white people came to South Africa, the country's wildlife species were abundant. Vast herds of wildebeests, zebras, and antelopes wandered the plains. One early white settler noted that it took a single herd of migrating springboks two days to pass a farm. During the 18th and early 19th centuries, white hunters

South Africa has 12 national parks as well as national game reserves and other protected wilderness areas. Many provide havens for the country's remarkable animals; others protect the country's beautiful landscapes.

33

The Kruger National Park

The Kruger National Park is the largest national park in the world. It covers a vast area in Northern and Mpumalanga provinces, totaling some 7,520 square miles (19,480 sq. km)—only slightly smaller than Massachusetts.

The park gets its name from Paul Kruger (1825–1904), an Afrikaner president of the South African Republic in the late 19th century. Kruger was a keen hunter rather than a conservationist. It is likely that the park's first warden, James Stevenson Hamilton, put Kruger's name forward in order to gain support for the project from Afrikaners. The government approved the idea in 1884, but it was only in 1898 that the area was set aside as a national park.

The park harbors a rich variety of wildlife, including 137 mammal, almost 500 bird, and more than 200 reptile species. For visitors, though, the park's main attraction is the chance of seeing the group of mammals known as the "Big Five"—elephants, lions, leopards, white rhinoceroses, and buffalos. The "Big Five" are among the most dangerous of Africa's animals. Hunters have always especially sought them out for their pelts and horns as trophies.

Leopards (shown below) are very shy and often hunt at night. Visitors to the park may be lucky enough to spot the fixed, yellowish-green eyes of a leopard as it rests in the cool of a rocky cliff.

The park has many other, smaller animals that are worth seeing, too. Antelope species such as the graceful impala, the blue wildebeest, and the shaggy waterbuck can be found throughout the park, as can zebras, giraffes, baboons, and vervet monkeys. The Olifants and Limpopo rivers, which flow through the park, are rich in birdlife.

stripped the Cape Provinces and Free State of their game herds, to clear the land for grazing, and for sport. By 1850, the Cape lion and the quagga, a relative of the zebra, were extinct.

During the late 19th century, some people began to see the need for conservation (protection of wildlife). In 1898, a vast tract of land on South Africa's eastern border was set aside as a protected area. Later, it became the Kruger National Park (*see* box opposite). Since the 1930s, the conservation movement has gathered force, and many reserves have been set up. Today, South Africa has 12 national parks and more than 300 private game reserves. No other African country has as well-managed or as rich a variety of reserves and parks.

Not all the national parks, however, are game reserves. Many are protected areas because of their dramatic landscapes or unusual plant life. Strict laws protect the native plants and animals. In recent years, South African conservationists have worked hard to protect threatened species such as the white and black rhinoceros (*see* box), elephant, lion, and leopard. In general, the future for South Africa's precious wildlife looks bright.

Africa's smallest frog, the micro frog, is found only in the Western Cape. The micro frog measures just $1/10$ inch (2 mm) long and is today an endangered species.

The White Rhinoceros Isn't White!

South Africa has two species of rhinoceros. The white, or square-lipped, rhinoceros is the larger, weighing up to 5,500 pounds (2,500 kg). Despite its name, the rhinoceros is not white at all but gray. Its name probably derives from a misunderstanding of the Afrikaans word *wijde*, meaning "wide," referring to the animal's broad, squarish lips. At the end of the 19th century, it was thought that the white rhinoceros was extinct. A few animals were discovered in Natal, however, and today, as a result of careful protection, there are 5,800.

The black rhinoceros is also gray in color but is much smaller than the white, weighing about 3,000 pounds (1,400 kg). There are fewer than 2,500 black rhinoceroses left in Africa, and the species is listed as endangered. The black rhinoceros is solitary and is hostile when disturbed, while the white rhinoceros is less threatening. Illegal hunting continues to threaten both species.

Many of South
Africa's places
have Afrikaans
as well as
English names.
For example,
Table Bay and
Lion's Head are
called *Tafelbaai*
and *Leeukop*
in Afrikaans.

SOUTH AFRICA'S CITIES

Black Africans traditionally lived in villages, sharing the surrounding pastureland. Settlements, however, often collected around a tribal stronghold. Since the late 17th century, European colonists have destroyed these African capitals and built their own settlements elsewhere.

Until the 20th century, South Africa's cities were very small. In 1865, even the biggest, Cape Town, had a population of just 40,000. Today, South Africa's urban population is much bigger and is concentrated in four main areas. The largest and most densely populated area is centered on Johannesburg, which stretches out about 45 miles (72 km) in all directions. Next biggest is Durban, followed by Cape Town and Port Elizabeth. In all South Africa's cities, there is a big difference between rich white neighborhoods and poor black ones (*see* pp. 106–107).

*Cable cars make the
trip to the summit
of Table Mountain
very easy. Once there,
there are spectacular
views of the city.*

Cape Town: At the Tip of Africa

Sheltered at the foot of the sheer, 3,563-feet-high (1,086 m) Table Mountain (*see* p. 12), Cape Town is one of the most beautiful cities in the world. Located near the southern tip of the African continent, it is also one of the most remote. Cape Town is South Africa's oldest town as

well, founded by Dutch settlers in 1652. The city became part of the British empire in 1806. The Afrikaans name for Cape Town is *Kaapstaad*, which has the same meaning.

The city has a dramatic natural setting. The city center—sometimes called the City Bowl—is flanked by Table Mountain to the south and by the heights of Lion's Head, Signal Hill, and Devil's Peak to the east and west. Clouds often gather on top of Table Mountain, forming a white, swirling "tablecloth." No visit to Cape Town is complete without a trip to the top of Table Mountain. Sightseers can walk or take the cable car. From the summit, there are panoramic views northward across the city to Table Bay and the Atlantic Ocean beyond. At noon every day, except Sunday, a cannon is fired from Signal Hill. The boom of the cannon can be heard throughout the town.

To the south of the city, beyond Table Mountain, stretches the Cape Peninsula. Here are wealthy suburbs, such as Camps Bay (*see* p. 24), beautiful beaches, and picturesque fishing villages. At the tip of the peninsula, 43 miles (70 km) south of the city center, is a nature reserve famous for its flowers. Most of the city's population lives in the sprawling suburbs to the east of Table Mountain. This often bleak area is known as the Cape Flats.

Offshore to the north lies Robben Island, which for many years was a penal (prison) colony. Its most famous prisoner was former president Nelson Mandela, who spent 27 years there. Robben Island was named for its seals, which are called *robbe* in Dutch. Close to the harbor, overlooking Table Bay, is the massive Castle of Good Hope. The castle is the oldest European building in

THE CAPE

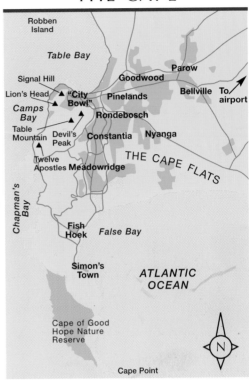

Downtown Cape Town contains historic buildings, museums, art galleries, gardens, and shopping malls. The outskirts of the city hold both rich suburbs, with luxury homes mainly for white people, and poor townships, formerly reserved for blacks.

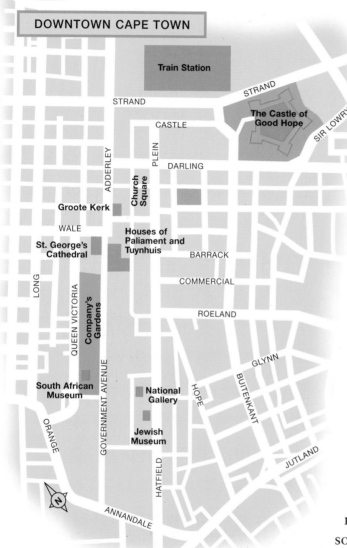

DOWNTOWN CAPE TOWN

Train Station

STRAND

STRAND

CASTLE

The Castle of Good Hope

SIR LOWRY

ADDERLEY

PLEIN

DARLING

Church Square

Groote Kerk

WALE

Houses of Paliament and Tuynhuis

BARRACK

St. George's Cathedral

COMMERCIAL

LONG

QUEEN VICTORIA

Company's Gardens

ROELAND

GLYNN

South African Museum

GOVERNMENT AVENUE

National Gallery

HOPE

BUITENKANT

ORANGE

Jewish Museum

JUTLAND

HATFIELD

N

ANNANDALE

A walk around Cape Town's downtown could take all day—there is so much to see! Today, the downtown is a vibrant meeting place for South Africa's many peoples and cultures.

South Africa. The first Dutch settlers built the castle to defend their colony. The castle is shaped like a pentagon, built with stout buttresses (external supports), to improve the fort's defenses.

To the west of the castle is Cape Town's downtown. The streets are based on a loose grid system, with roads crossing each other at right angles. One of the city's main thoroughfares is Adderley Street, which runs southwest from the harbor into the town and toward Table Mountain. Along its route are movie theaters, shops, cafés, restaurants, and a flower market, together with some of South Africa's oldest and most important buildings.

Groote Kerk ("Great Church") is the oldest church in South Africa and is the country's most important center for the Dutch Reformed Church. The original church was built in 1704, but today's building dates from 1841. Nearby is another important religious building—the Anglican (English Protestant) cathedral of St. George, built in 1901. Visitors go to marvel at its fine stained-glass windows, hear the choir sing, or listen to a sermon by South Africa's famous archbishop Desmond Tutu.

Beyond St. George's Cathedral, Adderley Street becomes Government Avenue. This handsome street contains many imposing buildings, including the Houses of Parliament (*see* p. 79) and the Tuynhuis ("town hall"), which dates from 1700. Today, the Tuynhuis is the residence of the South African president. Between Government Avenue and Queen Victoria Street are the Company's Gardens. The gardens, planted in the 17th century by the first Dutch settlers, contain 8,000 kinds of plants.

Nearby, the South African National Gallery holds some 7,000 works of art. On Hatfield Street, the Jewish Museum holds Jewish treasures. In the South African Museum, the prehistoric past is brought to life with huge dinosaur models and examples of San painting.

North of the city center, bordering Cape Town's busy harbor, lies the Victoria and Alfred Waterfront. This popular site contains the Two Oceans Oceanarium, and an Imax theater, as well as shops, markets, and museums.

The Cape Muslims

West of downtown is an old district of steep, cobbled streets, flat-topped houses, and mosques known as the Malay Quarter. This is the historic home of Cape Town's Muslim community, known as Cape Muslims or, by the whites, as Cape Malays. They are the descendants of slaves brought to the Cape Colony by the Dutch from their other colonies in Southeast Asia. The Cape Muslims used Malay as their shared language. Despite years of oppression, their community has remained vibrant.

The Victoria and Alfred Waterfront is packed with restaurants, bars, shops, and museums. It was named after the 19th-century British queen and her second son. The "Waterfront," as it is known, was Cape Town's original harbor, but was redeveloped in the early 1990s.

The Zulus call
Johannesburg
Egoli, meaning
"City of Gold."

Johannesburg: The City of Gold

Johannesburg is the capital of Gauteng Province and is South Africa's business capital. It lies at the crest of the Highveld, on the gold-rich Witwatersrand.

South Africa's largest city, Johannesburg, was built using revenues from gold. In 1886, a poor white prospector named George Harrison discovered gold on the Highveld. He sold his claim for $15, without realizing that he had discovered the surface outcrop of the world's richest gold reef. In under three years, a small mining camp of gold diggers had grown into the country's biggest city.

No one is certain how the city got its name, which means "John's Town." Some people say that it was named after Johann Rissik, the chief gold surveyor; others give the honor to Johannes Joubert, head of the mines department of the South African Republic in the late 19th century.

Today, the Johannesburg region is the source of 30 percent of the world's gold. Some of the world's richest and deepest gold mines lie below the city. On the surface, giant spoil heaps of earth proclaim the town's mining roots.

The metropolis of Johannesburg holds many contrasts. It is home to great extremes of wealth and poverty. In the city's downtown area, gleaming towers of glass and concrete soar upward, displaying the wealth of the town's mining corporations, banks, and businesses. Beyond the city's plush, white-dominated suburbs is a ring of black settlements, known as townships (*see* pp. 42–43), which are packed with basic, tin-roofed dwellings. There are few local amenities or even

The Johannesburg Memorial commemorates the miners who were among the city's first inhabitants.

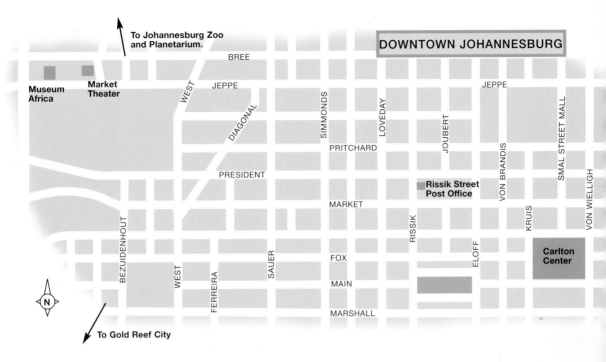

DOWNTOWN JOHANNESBURG

To Johannesburg Zoo and Planetarium.

Museum Africa

Market Theater

BREE

JEPPE

WEST

DIAGONAL

SIMMONDS

LOVEDAY

JOUBERT

JEPPE

VON BRANDIS

SMAL STREET MALL

PRITCHARD

PRESIDENT

Rissik Street Post Office

VON WIELLIGH

MARKET

RISSIK

KRUIS

BEZUIDENHOUT

WEST

SAUER

FOX

ELOFF

Carlton Center

FERREIRA

MAIN

MARSHALL

N

To Gold Reef City

supermarkets here. Yet for all their poverty, the black townships bubble with life and energy. The people of townships such as Soweto, Alexandra, and Sharpeville were the driving force behind many of the changes that have transformed South Africa in the last few years.

There is plenty to see in downtown Jo'burg. The city has dozens of open-air markets, art galleries and museums, movies, and theaters. The 50-story Carlton Center is a good place to begin sightseeing. At over 660 feet (200 m), this skyscraper is the tallest building in Africa. On its top floor is a viewing deck called the Top of Africa, from which there are fine views of the city. To the west lies the Johannesburg Stock Exchange, a striking, diamond-shaped building that gleams in the sun.

Northwest of the Carlton Center, the Market Theater Precinct has four theaters, many shops, and historic fruit and flower markets. Across the way, Museum Africa is a showcase for South African art, history, and culture, with dance displays and storytelling sessions. The Rissik Street Post Office, built in 1897, ranks as one of the oldest buildings in Johannesburg. Another story was added

Johannesburg's downtown (sometimes called the Central Business District, or CBD) is laid out on a simple grid. Under apartheid, Jo'burg's downtown was largely a white area; black South Africans were confined to the townships outside the city.

The Townships

When people speak of townships in the United States, they are usually referring to administrative divisions within a county. However, in South Africa a township is an urban area where black South Africans live. Until the end of apartheid in 1994, blacks, Asians, and coloreds (people of mixed race) were allowed to live only in townships. The townships often had populations of around 100,000. Soweto, South Africa's largest township, today has a population of around 600,000.

South Africa's white government introduced black townships in the early 1960s to help keep white and black South Africans separate. The townships were often

Unlike most cities or suburbs, townships did not grow slowly and of their own accord. Instead, they were carefully constructed according to rigid plans (above) in order to house a city's black manual workforce. As the photograph of Soweto shows (left), housing closely followed the linear design of these plans.

Despite the political instability and extreme poverty in some parts of the townships, most people there lead normal lives. Here, smartly dressed children in Alexandria Township, Johannesburg, make their way to school. Most children in the townships wear school uniforms.

built on the outskirts of big cities. In this way, the mines and factories in and around the cities had a supply of cheap black labor close at hand. In 1994, the laws forcing nonwhites to live in designated areas were abolished, and today everyone can live wherever they like as long as they can afford to pay for their houses. Nevertheless, townships remain mainly black areas.

Most white South Africans have little knowledge of townships, and few have been inside one. Many people imagine the townships to be dangerous, crime-ridden slums with unimaginable poverty. Although some parts are like this, other parts are not very different from suburbs anywhere.

In some parts of the townships are shanty areas where people live in shacks without bathrooms or running water. Most roads are not paved, and areas are not well kept by the local administration. One trash can is often shared by three or four families, so open places and roads are often littered with trash.

Despite the difficult living conditions and troubled history of the townships, white visitors are generally warmly greeted. Today, tourists can even visit the areas on organized tours.

The most famous and largest of South Africa's townships is Soweto (short for "South-Western Townships"), which lies south of Johannesburg. The Freedom Charter (*see* p. 69) was declared there in 1955, in the area called Freedom Square.

In June 1976, Soweto was the scene of a bloody massacre. In that year, the South African government ruled that black children had to be taught half of their lessons in Afrikaans. For many black people, this was the final straw. Thousands of black students took to the streets in Soweto to protest against the changes. The police fired on the marchers, killing more than 600 people, including many children. Black people in Soweto and all over South Africa rose up in outrage at the killings, and protests continued until 1994.

in 1902 to celebrate the coronation of King Edward VII of Great Britain. At the Planetarium to the north, visitors are able to find out all about the stars and planets that are visible in the Southern Hemisphere.

On the city outskirts is Johannesburg Zoo, which has some 3,000 different animals and a lake with rowboats for rent. Four miles (6 km) south of the downtown area is Gold Reef City, a theme park built on the site of some former mines. Visitors can descend the main shaft to view the machinery, see a reconstruction of 1890s Johannesburg, or watch molten gold being made into bars.

Durban: Surf City

The city and seaport of Durban is built around a large, almost landlocked lagoon called Natal Bay on the eastern coast of Africa. The weather here stays warm and sunny all year, and during the summer, the hot and humid climate can lead to heavy thunderstorms.

Durban's Juma Musjid Mosque, completed in 1927, is the largest mosque in the Southern Hemisphere. The mosque is the focal point of Durban's Indian district.

Durban was founded almost two centuries ago. In 1824, two British traders convinced a local Zulu king named Shaka (*see* p. 59) to give them some land to

set up a trading post on the coast. The British named the new settlement Durban after the governor of Britain's Cape Colony, Sir Benjamin D'Urban.

Later in the 19th century, Indian laborers arrived to work in the KwaZulu-Natal sugarcane fields. The sugarcane industry flourished, and Durban became its national headquarters. A railroad connecting Durban with the country's industrial heartland around Johannesburg was completed in 1895, and in 1904 Durban's harbor was opened up to large ships. These developments helped Durban become South Africa's main port.

Despite its heavy industry, Durban is also famous as a holiday resort. In summer, many South Africans head for Durban's 2 miles (6 km) of sandy beaches—the Golden Mile. Shark nets protect the warm waters for swimmers and surfers. The colorful, busy Marine Parade, which runs along the seafront, is the focus of the city. It is always crowded with tourists and Durbaners alike. A century ago, hundreds of rickshas carried passengers around the city; today, only a few remain, plying the seafront and adding to the exotic, holiday atmosphere.

The downtown is a vibrant mix of cultures. There are grand buildings in the British style, such as City Hall, as well as bustling Indian markets and a mosque and Hindu temple.

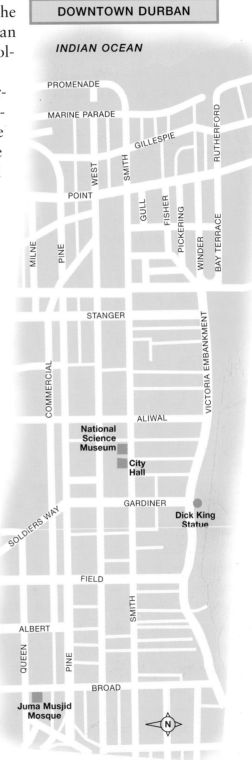

DOWNTOWN DURBAN

The Union Buildings overlook the city of Pretoria. The buildings are the South African government's administrative headquarters, but are located some distance from the downtown area.

Pretoria: The Boer Capital

In the province of Gauteng, only 35 miles (56 km) north of Johannesburg, is another important South African city—Pretoria. The SeSotho-speaking inhabitants of the city call it Tscwane.

Pretoria lies on a tributary of the Limpopo River in two sheltered valleys in the foothills of the Magaliesberg Mountains. Its relatively low altitude makes it warmer than Johannesburg. Summer temperatures range from 52–82 °F (15–28 °C), and even winters are mild and sunny.

The first European settlers in the area were the *voortrekkers* (*see* pp. 60–61), Afrikaner, or Boer, pioneers who migrated northward from the Cape Colony between 1836 and 1838. In 1855, the *voortrekker* leader Marthinus Wessels Pretorius (1819–1901) established a permanent settlement on the site. He named it after his father, the Boer hero of the Battle of Blood River, Andries Wilhelmus Pretorius (1798–1853). When the British recognized the independence of the Boer homeland north

The Voortrekker Monument

South of Pretoria is the huge Voortrekker Monument. Built in 1940, this striking monument commemorates the Boer victory over the Zulu in the Battle of Blood River (December 16, 1838). In the battle, 470 well-armed Boers defeated some 12,000 Zulus. Only three *voortrekkers* were wounded, while 3,000 Zulus were killed. Many Afrikaners consider the battle to be a decisive moment in their history. Each year, many Afrikaners make a pilgrimage to the spot on the battle's anniversary.

of the Vaal River, the town became the capital of a new Boer republic called the Transvaal Republic. The new republic was led by President Paul Kruger, who during the Anglo-Boer Wars resisted British attempts to take the country. The republic and Pretoria finally lost their independence to the British in 1902.

When the Union of South Africa was created in 1910, Pretoria became the administrative capital of the new country, a position it still holds today. Today, the government offices are housed in the distinctive Union Buildings, in an area northeast of the downtown known as Arcadia.

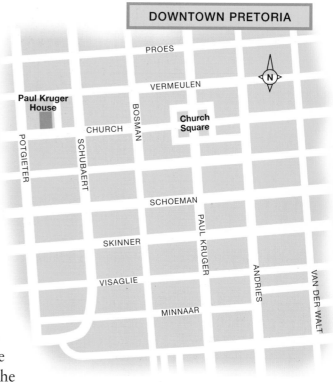

DOWNTOWN PRETORIA

At the heart of the modern city is Church Square. In earlier times, Boer farmers from the surrounding countryside gathered in the square at times of celebration. At the center of the square is a grim-looking statue of Paul Kruger. For many people, the statue of this uncompromising Boer hero is a reminder of the apartheid regime.

Running across the square from east to west is Church Street. More than 15 miles (25 km) long, it is one of the longest straight streets in the world. On Church Street, west of Church Square, is Paul Kruger House. The house was built in 1884 and is now a museum dedicated to Pretoria's most famous citizen.

Pretoria has a number of parks and gardens. A cable-car ride in the National Zoological Gardens, in the north of the city, provides fine views of the area.

Pretoria is built on a grid system. Long straight streets crisscross the city. At the center is the stately Church Square.

Past and Present

"The people shall govern."

First line of the ANC's Freedom Charter

Today, South Africa is the home of many different peoples. Its history is largely the story of how these peoples came to this beautiful country and of their struggle to assert their competing claims to its land and wealth. War, conflict, and oppression are the recurring themes of South Africa's tragic past.

The original inhabitants of the country were black African peoples, some of whom have lived on its lands for thousands of years. We know little of the ancient history of these peoples. Still, the remains of their tools and art can tell us something. Evidence suggests that successive waves of peoples brought new skills, lifestyles, and languages. Sometimes earlier native peoples were forced to move away to less fertile or drier lands; sometimes they adopted the newcomers' way of life.

In the 17th century, Europeans began to arrive in the country. They fought black Africans for their lands, destroying their societies and sometimes enslaving them. Bloody conflicts arose not only between blacks and whites but also among groups of Africans and Europeans.

South Africa became an independent country only in 1910. The new nation, however, was dominated by whites; blacks as well as other peoples had few or no rights. The history of 20th-century South Africa has been largely the story of the black struggle for freedom and equality and of the birth of a new and multiracial nation.

South Africa's former president Nelson Mandela was one of the greatest figures of the 20th century, admired all over the world for his integrity and courage.

FACT FILE

- The oldest fossil evidence of *Homo sapiens*—modern humans—was found in South Africa. Experts think that the fossils are the remains of humans who lived up to 100,000 years ago.

- South Africa was a colony—a country ruled and populated by another—for more than 250 years.

- With the election of Robert Mugabe as prime minister of Zimbabwe in 1980, South Africa became the last remaining white-controlled country in Africa.

- South Africa became a democracy only in 1994, with the first national nonracial elections.

ANCIENT TIMES

Scientists believe that hominids (upright, humanlike creatures) first developed in eastern and southern Africa some four million years ago. By about one million years ago, one species of hominid—*Homo erectus* ("standing man")—became dominant and spread throughout Africa and across the world, evolving into *homo sapiens* ("wise man"). These are the ancestors of all modern peoples.

The First Societies: The San

By about 30,000 years ago, the early humans of Southern Africa had formed small, simple societies. These early peoples are known as the San. The San roamed over a large part of Southern Africa, gathering nuts and berries and hunting animals such as antelopes with spears, bows, and arrows tipped with poison.

This San rock painting of an antelope is in South Africa's Eastern Cape Province.

The San were skilled desert survivors. They knew how to find water in springs hidden deep underground and carried the precious water in empty ostrich eggs. They painted simple line drawings or shaded silhouettes on the walls of caves or rock shelters. San rock art is found all over Southern Africa. The oldest paintings may date

NATIVE PEOPLES IN THE 18TH CENTURY

The first inhabitants of what is today South Africa were the Khoisan-speaking San and Khoikhoi. From A.D. 100, Nguni-speaking peoples came from the north, pushing the San and Khoikhoi to lands in the west and southwest. The map below shows where the black peoples of South Africa lived at around the time Europeans first came to the region.

San
The Khoisan-speaking San were the earliest inhabitants of South Africa. They were nomadic hunter-gatherers, but today very few survive.

Khoikhoi
The Khoisan-speaking Khoikhoi were known to the first European settlers as the Hottentots. They were nomadic herders, who lived in easily transportable, beehive-like huts.

Basuto
The southern Sotho—often called the Basuto—make up the modern population of the kingdom of Lesotho.

Tswana
The Tswana, also known as the Batswana, are a Sotho people. They gave their name to the country of Botswana, where many live.

Xhosa
Today, the majority of the Nguni-speaking Xhosa lives in southeasten South Africa. They are known as the "Red People" because of the red-dyed clothes worn by most adults.

Zulu
This Nguni-speaking people traditionally live in circular villages called *kraals*. Today, there are some six million Zulu in South Africa, making them the largest language group in the country.

Venda
This Nguni-speaking people migrated across the Limpopo River into the far northeast of South Africa in the 18th century. They are skillful ironworkers and are unusual in having female priests and avoiding pork in their diet.

Northern Sotho
The Nguni-speaking Northern Sotho live in the high grasslands of South Africa and include a large number of groups, including the Pedi and Lovedu. Their traditional villages (*kgoros*) are often quite large.

Ndebele
This Nguni-speaking people originally lived alongside the Zulu. In the 19th century, tribal wars forced them to migrate north to present-day Zimbabwe. They are skillfull craftspeople, making dazzling beadwork and copper jewelry.

from as long ago as 25,000 B.C., but many were made only in the 19th century. The paintings show people dancing or hunting animals, such as elephants, antelopes, and giraffes, and strange creatures that are half-animal, half-human (*see* p. 99).

Today, a few San still wander the Kalahari Desert, living in much the same way as their ancestors did thousands of years ago. The modern San are quite short and have light brown skin and dark curly hair. They do not own personal property, but share their possessions.

From Hunting to Herding

About 2,500 years ago, San living in the region to the north of South Africa became cattle- and sheep-herders. These people are known as the Khoikhoi ("men of men"), and, like the San, they speak a language known as Khoisan that includes tongue clicks. Gradually, the Khoikhoi moved their herds southward onto the High Veld and into the Cape region in search of fresh grazing land. There many San people also adopted the new arrivals' way of life and so became Khoikhoi, too.

The Khoikhoi herders lived in bigger groups than the San. The luckiest and most skillful members of the group acquired bigger herds, which they then passed on to their sons. The wealthiest herders might become leaders of a group. Sometimes groups led cattle raids on the herds of other groups in order to increase their wealth and therefore their power.

An early 19th-century German book on the peoples of Africa depicts a Nama man. The Nama are Khoikhoi cattle herders who today live around the lower reaches of the Orange River. They gave their name to the South African region of Namaqualand.

Farmers from the North

Some time after A.D. 100, tall, dark-skinned peoples from the north moved into eastern South Africa, pushing the Khoikhoi westward. The new peoples spoke Nguni, one of a branch of languages known as Bantu (*see* box opposite), and included the Zulu, Xhosa, and Ndebele. Other Nguni-speaking groups arrived during the 14th and 15th centuries or later. The Sotho and Tswana occupied parts of the central plateau, while the Tsonga settled in the west and the Venda in the northeast.

The newcomers generally lived more settled lives than the wandering San and Khoikhoi. They lived in settlements called *kraals* that sometimes included as many as 10,000 people. They grew crops, such as beans and millet, and kept cattle. They mined iron and copper to make weapons, tools, and ornaments, and traded salt and metals.

Nguni Society

In traditional Nguni society, men and women had different roles. Men herded cattle, cleared land for planting, and built the frames for houses. The women tended the crops, plastered the houses with cow dung, made pots or wove baskets, prepared the meals, and looked after the children.

Men often had several wives. When a woman married, her new husband gave her family cattle in return. This payment in cattle is known as *bridewealth*. Sometimes bridewealth was not paid until the new wife had given birth to a male heir. The number of wives a man had showed his wealth.

Unlike the San, who lived in small groups without official leaders, the farming peoples were often led by kings. The kings grew powerful by making cattle raids or by winning the loyalty of more people. Marriage was the usual way of forming new alliances. A king sometimes ruled from a mighty fortress.

The king's main responsibility was to ensure the prosperity of his people. Above all, this meant making sure that rain fell to nourish the crops. Drought was blamed on the bad behavior of individuals or the angry spirits of ancestors, and it was the king's job to make sure the guilty were punished and offerings were made to the ancestors.

Native Languages

There are more than 1,700 languages spoken in Africa. Linguists (language experts) divide them into four language "families." A language family is a group of languages that share common origins. Two language families are found in South Africa—Khoisan and Niger-Kordofanian. Khoisan is spoken by the San and the Khoikhoi, and its most unusual feature is a clicking sound that appears before almost every word. The Niger-Kordofanian languages spoken in South Africa all belong to the Bantu branch of the family and include the Nguni languages spoken by the Zulu, Xhosa, and Sotho peoples. Some Bantu languages, such as Xhosa and Zulu, are mutually intelligible, although many others are not. Some Nguni languages have adopted the clicks of Khoisan.

THE FIRST WHITE SETTLERS

In the late 15th century, white Europeans began to explore the southwest coast of Africa. In 1485, the Portuguese navigator Diogo Cão (1450–1486) sailed as far south as Cape Cross in present-day Namibia, where he set up a stone pillar in honor of the Portuguese king. Cão never returned to Portugal, and historians assume that he was shipwrecked on the voyage home.

TO THE CAPE

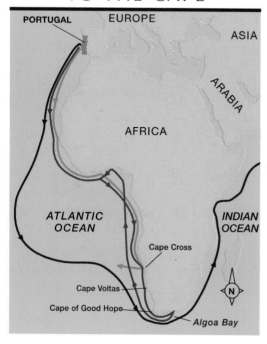

Route of Diogo
Cão (1485)

Route of
Bartolomeu Dias
(1487–1488)

Route of Vasco
da Gama
(1497–1499)

In the late 15th century, Portuguese explorers began to search for a sea passage to the East. In 1498, Vasco da Gama (about 1460–1524) crowned Cão's and Dias's epic voyages by reaching India.

Rounding the Cape

Two years later, Portugal's king sent another navigator, Bartolomeu Dias (around 1450–1500), on a mission to reach the southernmost tip of Africa. The king was eager to find a sea route to the Indies because wars had disrupted the overland routes through Central Asia.

After four months, Dias and his fellow explorers passed the stone pillar left by Cão and reached the mouth of the Orange (Gariep) River, just to the north of present-day South Africa. Shortly after, the Portuguese ships met a terrible storm that blew them southward for 13 days. Eventually, Dias made landfall on an island in Algoa Bay, not realizing that he had in fact rounded the tip of Africa. Dias sailed for a few more days before giving in to his crew's pleas to turn around and head for home. It was only on the return voyage that Dias spotted the cape, which he named the Cape of Good Hope.

By the early 17th century, European ships were regularly rounding the Cape on trading missions to India and the Far East. At about the halfway mark on these long voyages, the Cape of Good Hope was a good place to refuel, offering water and the chance of obtaining fresh meat through trade with the Khoikhoi. The strategic importance of the Cape was obvious to both the Dutch and British, but it was the Dutch who acted decisively.

The Dutch Colony

In 1652, a Dutch trading organization called the Dutch East India Company sent an expedition led by Jan van Riebeeck (1619–1677) to set up a supply base at the Cape. Where the city of Cape Town stands today, van Riebeeck built a fort and planted a garden to grow fresh fruit and vegetables (*see* box). He also planted an almond hedge to mark off the new Dutch territory.

People who worked for the company were soon allowed to settle in the region beyond the fort and farm their own plots of land. They called themselves *Boers*, the Dutch word for "farmers." The Boers used slaves to do their heavy work. Some slaves were African, but most were imported from India, Malaysia, and other Asian countries. By the end of the 18th century, there were some 15,000 slaves working in the colony.

Oranges

On his way to the Cape Colony, its first governor, Jan van Riebeeck, stopped on the island of St. Helena, in the South Atlantic Ocean. There he tasted an orange for the first time and was so taken with the delicious fruit that he took some of the seeds with him to plant at the Cape. The oranges flourished in the sunny climate, and they soon became a staple of the settlers' diet. Later, Dutch and British pioneers often took oranges on their long treks inland.

The settlement founded on the Cape at Table Bay was a welcome sight for sailors on the long, difficult trip to and from the Indies.

Almost from the beginning, the Khoikhoi and San resisted the Dutch attempts to take their land. Their spears and bows, however, were no match for the Dutch guns and swords. The Dutch killed hundreds of native people, kidnapped their children, and raided their flocks and herds. In one such raid in 1674, the Dutch seized some 800 cattle and 4,000 sheep. One San leader bitterly complained: "What are you doing in my land? You have taken all the places where the eland [a type of antelope] and other game live. Why did you not stay where the sun goes down, where you first came from?"

During the late 17th century, a steady stream of white settlers arrived to swell the numbers of Europeans at the Cape. They included Dutch, Germans, and French Protestants, called Huguenots, who were fleeing religious persecution in their own countries. The Europeans settled on lands inhabited by the Khoikhoi.

In the wars of the 1670s, the Europeans' superior weapons enabled them to defeat the Africans. Some Khoikhoi became servants of the Dutch. Others returned

Jan van Riebeeck, founder of the Cape Colony, meets representatives of the Khoikhoi. This 19th-century painting suggests that the Dutch occupation of native lands was the result of negotiation, not brutal warfare.

EARLY CAPE SETTLEMENTS c.1690

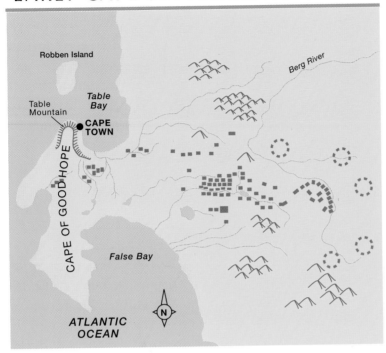

▪ Dutch and Huguenot farms

⬚ Khoikhoi *kraals*

⛰ Mountains

After the 1670s, settlers on the Cape were able to set up farms on the plains east of the Dutch fort. The farmers planted vines and wheat and used both native and imported slaves to work the fields. After 1690, poorer settlers known as trekboers began to search for new pasture-lands farther north and east, where they met stiff resistance from African peoples.

to the nomadic life of the San hunters and waged a guerrilla war against the settlers. Many native people died of diseases brought by the Europeans, such as smallpox and measles. Eventually, the Khoikhoi became almost extinct.

The Colony Grows

During the 18th century, white settlement spread inland from the southwestern tip of South Africa. Poor Dutch ranchers called *trekboers* ("trek farmers") roamed hundreds of miles inland in search of pastures for their cattle. Wherever they went, they took away land from the San and Khoikhoi and forced many to work for them. Along the frontiers of the expanding Cape Colony, they came into conflict with African peoples such as the Xhosa.

The settlers also had a devastating impact on the Cape environment. Their large herds grazed on the lands formerly lived on by native animals. Some species, such as the blauwbok antelope and the quagga zebra, died out.

BRITISH, ZULU, AND BOERS

In 1795, Britain occupied the Cape to strengthen its grip over the trade routes to India. In 1803, the British returned the colony to the Dutch, only to seize it back again in 1806. The Cape Colony formally became part of the British empire in 1820, and thousands of British settlers arrived to settle there. The British introduced some reforms, but left much unchanged, leaving, for example, the Dutch legal system in place.

During the 19th century, powerful African kingdoms emerged in Southern Africa. The kingdoms fiercely resisted the European settlers but were eventually subdued. Some of the kingdoms, such as those of the Sotho and the Swazi, are the origin of modern African nations.

The Rise of the Zulu

The 19th century was a time of conflict among African groups. In the 1820s, a fierce Zulu king named Shaka (about 1787–1828) won a great empire for his people in the area today known as KwaZulu-Natal (*see* box opposite). Thousands of Africans fled inland to escape the terror of his armies. This forced migration is known as the Difaqane or Mfecane. The fleeing peoples fought for new lands on the Highveld. Experts estimate that more than two million people died in the struggles that followed.

Other leaders used the chaos created by the Zulu to build their own kingdoms. North of Shaka's territory, the Ndebele, under a rebellious Zulu general called Mzilikazi, carved out their own kingdom in what is now Botswana. In the southern Highveld, the Sotho king Moshoeshoe established a mountain kingdom through a clever mix of diplomacy and military tactics (*see* p. 22). These and other African kingdoms lasted until the 1870s.

AFRICAN KINGDOMS

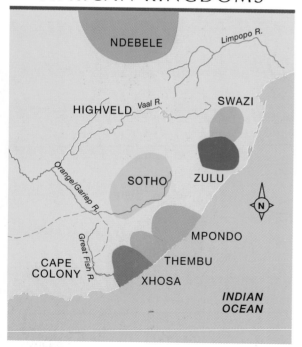

NDEBELE
Limpopo R.
HIGHVELD Vaal R.
SWAZI
Orange/Gariep R.
SOTHO ZULU
N
MPONDO
Great Fish R.
THEMBU
CAPE COLONY
XHOSA
INDIAN OCEAN

Shaka's Armies

Shaka was the son of the Zulu king Senzangakona and a princess from a neighboring people. At the beginning of the 19th century, the Zulu were one of the smallest of the Bantu-speaking peoples, numbering only some 1,500 people. Their homeland lay in what is today known as KwaZulu-Natal.

Shaka became the Zulu king in 1816. He was determined to build a mighty empire. He reorganized the Zulu army, creating highly trained army units called *impi*s. African warriors traditionally fought with oxhide shields and spears. Once thrown, the spear was lost and the warrior became useless. Shaka's warriors adopted a short, deadly spear, called an *assegai*, which they used for hand-to-hand fighting. Warriors also hardened their feet by treading on thorns, so they could race across the countryside at great speed. This Zulu warrior (right) was Shaka's nephew Utimuni.

When going into battle, *impi* units formed a shape like an ox. While the strongest warriors (the "chest") attacked the enemy from the front, two other units—the "horns"—outflanked and surrounded the enemy.

Using these crack forces, Shaka was able to defeat all the neighboring peoples along the coast. Thousands of Africans fled inland, while many others joined forces with the Zulu, swelling Shaka's empire.

In 1827, Shaka's mother died, and in a fit of madness, he began killing his own people. In 1828, two of Shaka's half brothers murdered the king. The Zulu empire, however, survived and remained a powerful force through the 19th century.

The Great Trek

The Boers deeply resented British rule. The ill-feeling was partly about the two groups' different attitudes to black Africans. The Boers treated their black slaves very harshly and quoted the Bible to support their belief that black people were destined to serve whites. The British, by contrast, tended to treat the native population with more respect.

In 1834, tensions came to a head when the British abolished slavery throughout the British empire. Many Boers decided that it was time to free themselves from their meddlesome new rulers. Between 1836 and 1838, some 10,000 Boers left Cape Colony and headed north and east in search of new lands and independence. With their cattle herds and black servants, the *voortrekkers* (pioneers) traveled thousands of miles across rough country in ox-drawn wagons. The Boers' epic journey became known as the Great Trek.

At first, the *voortrekkers* settled in the grasslands around the Vaal River, forcing the area's Ndebele inhabitants northward. A few small farming communities, or *dorps*, were set up in the area. The majority of the *voortrekkers*, however, turned southeastward, crossing the Drakensberg into what is now KwaZulu-Natal. Here they came into conflict with the mighty Zulu kingdom. The *voortrekkers* had developed an effective defense against attack, setting their wagons in a close, protective circle, or *laager*, within which they set up camp. In 1838, under the leadership of Andries

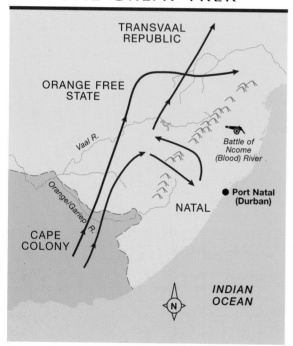

THE GREAT TREK

TRANSVAAL REPUBLIC

ORANGE FREE STATE

Vaal R.

Battle of Ncome (Blood) River

Orange/Gariep R.

NATAL

Port Natal (Durban)

CAPE COLONY

INDIAN OCEAN

N

From 1836, thousands of Boer pioneers, later known as voortrekkers, *left Cape Colony in search of new lands to the north and east.*

Pretorius (1798–1853), they defeated the Zulu at the Battle of Ncome River (later called the Battle of Blood River) and asserted their rule over much of the region.

In 1842, the British, who had a settlement on the coast at Port Natal (later Durban), claimed the Boers' new homeland, Natal, for themselves. The Boers were forced to move on again. Pretorius led his people back to the Highveld. Arriving in the wake of the Difaqane, to their surprise they found the land empty of people.

During the 1850s, the Boers established two republics, the Orange Free State and, in the north, the Transvaal (or South African Republic). At first, the British were prepared to recognize the new Boer states. However, their attitude quickly changed when they discovered that the new Boer lands contained great mineral riches.

The Battle of Blood River is so called because the waters of the river where the battle took place were reddened by the blood of thousands of Zulus.

Gold and Diamond Fever

In 1866, a 15-year-old boy discovered a shiny white diamond on the banks of the Orange (Gariep) River near Hopetown, about 75 miles (120 km) southwest of present-day Kimberley. More diamonds were discovered along the Vaal and Orange rivers during 1867–1868. Then, in 1870, another rich diamond field was discovered at a small hill called Colesberg Koppie, which later became Kimberley. The finds triggered the biggest diamond rush in history. Thousands of prospectors rushed to the area, mainly from Britain, hoping to strike it rich. By 1872, there were some 50,000 people living in the area.

In 1886, a poor white prospector named George Harrison found traces of gold in the Witwatersrand region of the Transvaal.

Miners in Kimberley, Orange Free State, extract diamonds from the earth. By the mid-1870s, Kimberley was the second-largest settlement in South Africa.

SOUTH AFRICA IN AROUND 1900

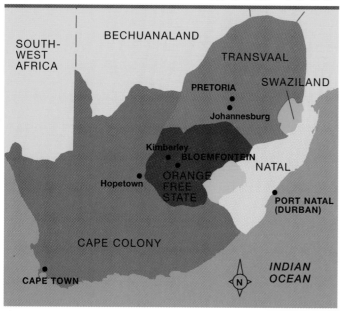

SOUTH-WEST AFRICA

BECHUANALAND

TRANSVAAL

PRETORIA

SWAZILAND

Johannesburg

Kimberley

BLOEMFONTEIN

Hopetown

ORANGE FREE STATE

NATAL

PORT NATAL (DURBAN)

CAPE COLONY

CAPE TOWN

INDIAN OCEAN

N

By 1890, the land that later became South Africa was divided between the Boer republics— Transvaal and Orange Free State—and the British colonies— Cape Colony and Natal. Other territories were British protectorates— African kingdoms that recognized the authority of the British empire.

Soon it became clear that vast deposits of gold lay beneath the ground in the area, and gold prospectors began flocking to the Witwatersrand.

The British government then tried to seize control of the gold-rich Boer lands. It claimed that it wanted to protect the interests of the British inhabitants of the Boer republics, who were known as *uitlanders* ("outlanders"). Hostility between the Boers and the British finally erupted in open war from 1880 to 1881 and again from 1899 to 1902.

The South African War

By 1900, more than 200,000 British soldiers were fighting against the Boers, whose total population was only 300,000. The Boers put up a stout defense, digging trenches and using modern weapons, such as rapid-fire Mauser rifles, against the enemy. In June, however, the British overran the Orange Free State and occupied the town of Johannesburg in the Transvaal mining region.

The Boers fought on, adopting guerrilla tactics. In response, the British burned and looted Boer farms and imprisoned thousands of Boer families and their black workers in concentration camps. Up to 27,000 Boers and 14,000 black Africans died of diseases in the camps. The brutal methods used by the British caused great bitterness among the Afrikaners ("Africans"), as the Boers had come to be known. In 1902, Britain annexed the two Boer republics as two new British colonies.

Wealth and Oppression

Meanwhile, the new mining industry had brought great changes to both blacks and whites in South Africa. Great riches lay underground, but at such great depths that small-scale prospectors could not reach them. Only major companies employing large numbers of workers could mine effectively.

Within a short time, a few large companies, such as De Beers Consolidated Mines, controlled all the gold and diamond fields. The men who worked in the mines were paid very low wages and had to work in terrible conditions. In the early years of the industry, local Africans did not want to work as miners, so large numbers of laborers were brought in from neighboring countries, such as Mozambique; some even came from China. In Natal, too, Indian laborers had been imported since the 1860s to work in white-owned factories and sugar plantations.

Gandhi in South Africa

The great Indian statesman Mahatma Gandhi (1869–1948) trained as an attorney. As a young man, Gandhi (center) practiced law in South Africa, parts of which were, like India, part of the British empire. In 1893, Gandhi bought a first-class ticket for a train journey to Johannesburg but was ordered into the third-class carriage. At that time, only white people were allowed to travel first class in South Africa. Gandhi protested and was thrown off the train.

The incident was crucial to the development of his ideas about peaceful resistance to white supremacy. In South Africa, Gandhi began to fight for the rights of Indian workers, and in 1913 he led a peace march. Later, he returned to India and used the principal of nonviolent opposition in his campaign to win India's independence from Britain in 1947.

In late January 1879, some 10,000 Zulu warriors—supporters of the Zulu king Cetewayo (about 1826–1884)—carried out a surprise attack on invading British and native troops at their camp near Isandhlwana east of the Buffalo River in Zululand. The British were forced to retreat, losing many men as they did so. A party of British troops managed to flee west to a ford at Rourke's Drift, hoping to escape across the Buffalo River. There they made a final, brave stand.

During the late 1800s, the British passed new laws that put pressure on Africans to work for the whites. As one method of forcing Africans to cooperate, the British government introduced a "hut tax," payable on African homes. To earn the money needed to pay the tax, many Africans were forced into paid work for the first time. Many Africans left their lands and families to live far away in crowded, insanitary housing compounds near the mines.

The Zulu Wars

During the late 19th century, the whites continued to seize new lands from the African peoples. Tribes such as the Zulu, Xhosa, and Ndebele resisted fiercely, but were finally defeated. In 1879, the Zulu won a great victory over the British at the Battle of Isandhlwana. Zulu warriors attacked the invading British force, killing 1,800 soldiers. In later battles, however, they too were overwhelmed by superior British weapons.

By 1900, the traditional way of life for most black Africans had been destroyed, and many thousands of native people had been uprooted. In 1906, the Zulu chief Bambatha led the last armed rebellion. The British crushed the revolt, and 4,000 Zulus died.

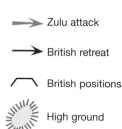

Zulu attack

British retreat

British positions

High ground

BATTLE OF ISANDHLWANA

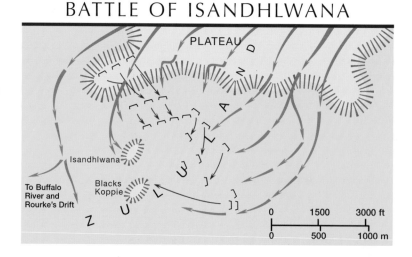

THE UNION OF SOUTH AFRICA

In the early 1900s, British and Afrikaners began talks aimed at ending their differences and forming a united country. Black Africans were given no say in the future of this new country. On May 31, 1910, the two former Boer republics of Orange Free State and Transvaal and the British colonies of Cape and Natal merged to form the Union of South Africa, a self-governing nation within the British empire.

White Rulers, Black Country

The new country gave hardly any rights to blacks and people of mixed race, who were known as "coloreds." At the time of the formation of the Union, blacks made up some four million of a total population of just under six million. Whites numbered about 1.2 million; 600,000 were colored; while another 150,000 were Indian.

Jan Smuts was one of the principal founders of the Union of South Africa. He served both as deputy prime minister and as prime minister and retired from politics only in 1948, at the age of 78.

A new party called the South African National Party, made up of various Boer groups, won the first election and formed the government. The party soon became known as the South African Party, or SAP. Both the prime minister, Louis Botha (1862–1919), and his deputy, Jan Smuts (1870–1950), were pro-British Afrikaners who worked to reconcile British and Afrikaner interests. Nonwhites had no democratic rights.

The new government set out to consolidate all the gains that whites had won in the previous century. In 1913, a new law called the Natives Land Act made the seizure of black lands legal. By law, black Africans could own land only in the 10 percent of the country that was reserved for them. All the rest of the land was set aside for whites.

THE UNION OF SOUTH AFRICA

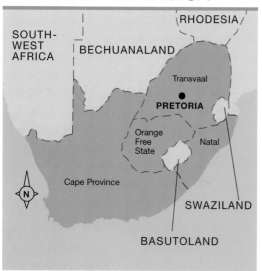

The Union of South Africa came into being on May 31, 1910. The four former colonies formed the country's new provinces, with Pretoria as the capital. The British territories of Basutoland (Lesotho), Bechuanaland (Botswana), Swaziland, and Rhodesia (Zimbabwe) did not join the Union. In 1915, the Union seized South-West Africa (Namibia).

Black Protest

In protest at this new stage of white domination, some black Africans formed a political organization called the South African Native National Congress (SANNC). Later, in 1925, the SANNC was renamed the African National Congress (ANC). The ANC was mostly made up of educated men and women who believed they could win rights for blacks through sheer force of reason.

SANNC leaders, such as Sol Plaatje (1877–1932) and the Reverend John Dube (1871–1946), visited Europe and North America to draw attention to the situation in South Africa. SANNC delegates visited Britain to seek "equal rights for all civilized men," but their requests fell on deaf ears. The British government was happy to leave South African affairs in the hands of its government.

Some Afrikaners wanted full independence for South Africa. In 1914, General Barry Hertzog (1866–1942) formed the National Party. The party supported independence from Britain, segregation between whites and blacks and coloreds, and Afrikaner rights.

South Africa during the World Wars

The South African government continued to be pro-British. When World War I broke out in Europe in 1914, Prime Minister Botha led South Africa into the war against Germany. The war boosted South Africa's economy. Between the 1910s and 1950s, the country became a modern, industrial nation. Many changes deepened the gulf between black and white. Rapid industrialization and the new laws dispossessed more blacks, forcing them to leave the countryside and seek work in towns.

During the following years, legislation was passed that further discriminated against nonwhites in South Africa. In 1923, a new act stated that blacks in towns could only live in certain areas. In 1936, another land act based on the Natives Land Act of 1913 created a divided country where whites owned 87 percent of the land.

However, even these harsh measures were not enough to satisfy some Afrikaners. In the 1930s, white extremists led by D.F. Malan (1874–1959) formed a new political group, the Purified National Party. In the years leading up to World War II, this group won increasing support among white South Africans.

World War II broke out in 1939. Jan Smuts, now prime minister, again led South Africa to support Britain and the Allies, but this move was unpopular with many Afrikaners. During the war years, the Purified National Party gained more support, and in the 1948 election, it swept to victory as the first all-Afrikaner government of the Union.

THE APARTHEID YEARS

The new government set out to reshape South African society entirely for the benefit of whites. Over the next few years, major new laws created a system of enforced racial segregation (keeping people of different races apart). It was known as "apartheid," which means "separateness" in Afrikaans, the Afrikaner language.

In 1950, the Population Registration Act classified all South Africans as one of four "racial groups": whites, Africans, Asians, and coloreds. The new classifications affected all aspects of people's lives: their freedom of movement, where they could live, whom they could

Black workers board a crowded black-only bus in Johannesburg. Under apartheid, black and white South Africans were forced to lead separate lives.

Dr. Hendrik Verwoerd

The man responsible for setting up apartheid was South Africa's Afrikaner minister of native affairs, Dr. Hendrik Verwoerd (1902–1966). Verwoerd was a brilliant psychologist and philosopher, and a fanatical believer in the God-given privileges of the Afrikaner nation. In 1958, he became South Africa's prime minister and continued to impose his extremist views on his country. In 1966, he was stabbed to death as he sat in parliament.

The colors of the ANC flag are black, green, and gold. The ANC adopted the flag in 1925.

marry, and the work they could do. Blacks were barred from some well-paid jobs. Different races had separate schools, separate places to live, and separate shops. Blacks and whites were not allowed to sit on the same park bench, ride in the same bus, or even be buried in the same cemetery.

The situation became even more extreme in 1952 when new Pass Laws decreed that all Africans had to carry a pass (identity card) in white areas. If they could not produce their pass on demand, they could be arrested and detained.

The Cry for Freedom

In the 1950s, opposition to these harsh new laws united under the banner of the African National Congress (ANC). Support for the organization had been growing steadily since the 1920s. During the 1940s, young black activists, including Oliver Tambo (1917–1993) and Nelson Mandela (born 1918), had become convinced that the ANC's polite requests for change would never alter the government's course. They formed the ANC Youth League, which called for a more radical campaign against apartheid.

Soon the main body of the ANC saw the force of the Youth League's arguments. In 1952, the ANC initiated a program of mass action, known as the "Defiance Campaign," which included strikes, marches, and civil disobedience, to protest against apartheid. Thousands of people joined in the campaign and broke the new laws, and 8,000 were arrested.

From the 1950s, the government voted itself new powers to enforce apartheid and silence protesters. Its actions only convinced thousands more to join opposition groups such as trade unions, the South African Communist Party (SACP), and the ANC. In 1955, the ANC and other protest groups came together to form the Congress Alliance.

At a meeting attended by 3,000 delegates from all races, the alliance put forward its Freedom Charter, a blueprint for a just society (*see* box). The charter demanded that all South Africans should share in their country's wealth and land, and that all should have equal rights. The government acted swiftly, banning the charter and arresting Congress leaders. The message of the charter—notably the slogan, "The people shall govern"—was a powerful rallying cry for freedom.

The Sharpeville Massacre

The year 1960 was a turning point for South Africa. In March, some 5,000 people gathered in Sharpeville, a black township outside Johannesburg, to protest against the Pass Laws. The police opened fire on the unarmed demonstrators, killing 69 people and wounding 187 others.

Many countries condemned the government's action. In reply, South Africa left the Commonwealth (a group of self-governing states that pledges allegiance to the British crown). The country became a republic in May 1961, turning its back on the world. The ANC and another group, the Pan Africanist Congress (PAC), called for a new wave of protest. The government responded by banning the ANC and the PAC.

The Freedom Charter

The Congress of the People was held near Johannesburg in 1955. The Freedom Charter—a ten-point manifesto for a new South Africa drafted by Lionel Bernstein—was adopted at the congress. It reads as follows:

The people shall govern.
All national groups shall have equal rights.
The people shall share the nation's wealth.
The land shall be shared by those who work it.
All shall be equal before the law.
All shall enjoy equal human rights.
There shall be work and security for all.
The doors of learning and culture shall be opened.
There shall be houses, security, and comfort.
There shall be peace and friendship.

The Armed Struggle

Since 1912, the ANC had tried to negotiate change within South Africa by peaceful means. Since they were officially banned, ANC and PAC activists now chose to organize armed resistance to apartheid in secret. Mandela and other activists launched a new organization, *Umkhonto we Sizwe* (MK for short)—the Spear of the Nation. The group began to bomb targets that symbolized white rule.

In 1963, Mandela, Walter Sisulu, and other MK leaders were arrested. At their trial, they argued the case for a nonracial South Africa with great eloquence, but were sentenced to life imprisonment for treason. With most of its leaders in prison, the resistance movement was dead inside South Africa for ten years. In exile, however, ANC leaders, such as Oliver Tambo, continued the struggle, encouraging international opposition to apartheid.

In 1959, the prime minister, Hendrik Verwoerd, introduced another repressive measure. This was the Promotion of Bantu Self-Government Act. Under this

The 1959 Promotion of Bantu Self-Government Act created ten homelands, or bantustans, for South Africa's black population. Each homeland was reserved for a separate "nationality." Millions of people assigned to these nationalities were forced to resettle in the homelands, often located in dry, remote areas.

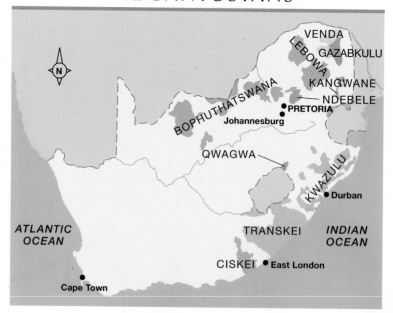

THE BANTUSTANS

VENDA
LEBOWA
GAZABKULU
KANGWANE
BOPHUTHATSWANA
NDEBELE
PRETORIA
Johannesburg
QWAGWA
KWAZULU
Durban
ATLANTIC OCEAN
TRANSKEI
INDIAN OCEAN
CISKEI East London
Cape Town

Steve Biko was an inspiration to millions of black men and women. During the 1970s, he set up the South African Students Association and the Black Peoples Convention, which together fostered the Black Consciousness Movement. This mural, painted in South Africa in 1994, commemorates Biko's life and death.

act, the lands reserved for black people were divided into ten *bantustans*, or "homelands." Africans could only live in these homelands or in the black townships around the major cities and industrial areas. By making black people citizens of the homelands, the government could continue to deny them rights in South Africa itself.

During the 1970s, four of the home-lands—Transkei, Bophuthatswana, Venda, and Ciskei—received a form of independence, with their own "governments." But the United Nations (UN) did not recognize the homelands as true nations.

Black Consciousness

During the 1970s, a wave of new ideas swept the townships and black colleges. The Black Consciousness Movement created a new pride in being black. One of the leaders of the new movement was Steve Biko (1946–1977). In 1977, Biko died while being held by the police. The medical

Namibia

In the late 19th century, the arid country today known as Namibia was a German colony known as South-West Africa. During World War I, South Africa seized the country as part of the Allied campaign against Germany. South Africa held on to the territory after the war, and, despite international opposition, tried to make it part of the Union. In 1968, the United Nations (UN) recognized the country as Namibia, although full independence was achieved only in 1990.

report showed that he had died of massive blows to the head. Some 15,000 Africans attended his funeral together with representatives from 13 nations.

Steve Biko is remembered today for the inspiration he gave to all black South Africans living under apartheid. He believed that if black people thought better of themselves, whites would find it harder to oppress them.

The Beginning of Reform

From 1978 to 1990, the ruling National Party was led by Pieter Willem Botha (born 1916). In the early 1980s, in response to international criticism, the government created two new houses of parliament, for Indians and coloreds. Botha also passed laws that gave Indians and coloreds the right to vote. However, since both the new houses could be overruled by the white parliament in South Africa and black Africans were still not able to vote, most people condemned the move as a sham.

In 1983, major protest groups, such as the United Democratic Front (UDF), began to organize strikes and marches. In exile, the ANC called for a new wave of action to make the townships "ungovernable." Protests continued for three years. Altogether 3,000 resisters were killed, and 30,000 were arrested. The government declared a state of emergency, which gave the police and army new powers to suppress the tide of protest.

The Inkatha Freedom Party flag consists of seven horizontal stripes of red, white, black, green, yellow, white, and red. The middle three stripes are the colors of the ANC, showing the two groups' earlier alliance.

Meanwhile, conflict spread among the black groups opposing apartheid. The Inkatha Freedom Party (IFP), a Zulu-dominated organization led by Chief Mangosotho Buthelezi, disagreed with ANC methods of fighting apartheid (*see* box opposite). From 1984 on, clashes between supporters of the two groups became more frequent. The government gave financial assistance to Inkatha in an attempt to split black opposition, and many extremist whites encouraged these conflicts.

The Inkatha Freedom Party

The Zulu homeland in KwaZulu-Natal was dominated by the Inkatha Freedom Party (IFP) and its leader, Mangosotho Buthelezi. Buthelezi founded the IFP in 1975 to fight against apartheid. By the early 1990s, the party was the largest in South Africa, with some two million members. As chief minister of KwaZulu, Buthelezi came to believe that the best way to improve black rights was to work with the South African government.

The party was dominated by rural Zulus. Some of its followers modeled themselves on the *impis*, the fierce bands of warriors who fought for Shaka in the 19th century. Support for the IFP was confined mainly to the countryside. In cities such as Durban, blacks supported more radical groups such as the ANC. The ANC was critical of Buthelezi, arguing that he was a collaborator with the South African regime.

THE END OF APARTHEID

By the late 1980s, the apartheid system had reached a breaking point. The whole country was in turmoil, and there was chaos in the townships. Overseas, the trickle of encouragement for the ANC had grown into a great tide of support. An age of reform and openness was dawning in the Soviet Union, eastern Europe, and elsewhere. By contrast, South Africa seemed determined to stick with its repressive and unfair system of apartheid in the face of international opposition.

Nelson Mandela

Nelson Rolihlahla Mandela was born in Transkei, in the Eastern Cape, in 1918. He trained as a lawyer and, with Oliver Tambo, set up South Africa's first black law firm. During the 1940s and 1950s, he organized the activities of the ANC Youth League. After the ANC was banned in 1961, he went "underground" and helped to organize the armed struggle against apartheid. In 1963, he was arrested and sentenced to life imprisonment.

Mandela was imprisoned on Robben Island, a desolate island in Table Bay. There he became a symbol of the fight for freedom. During the apartheid years, his fame grew despite the fact that, as a banned person, his words could not be quoted nor his picture displayed. Supporters could be arrested for merely wearing a "Free Mandela" T-shirt.

Meanwhile, Robben Island became known as "the university of the struggle," as Mandela educated other prisoners in the ANC's beliefs. Even the prison guards had to be changed often, as they were swayed by Mandela's arguments. Mandela was finally released at the age of 71 on February 11, 1990. He later became South Africa's first black president. On December 31, 1999, Mandela revisited his cell in Robben Island prison (above).

After her husband's arrest, Nelson Mandela's wife, Winnie (born 1934), was for many years a key figure in the antiapartheid campaign. Her popularity waned when she was accused of having black youths beaten for political reasons. One youth died as a result of his injuries. Partly as a result of these accusations, the Mandelas separated in 1992.

Trouble at Home and Abroad

In 1986, the United States, the European Community (EC), and the British Commonwealth imposed trade sanctions (bans) on South Africa in protest against apartheid. No weapons were sold to the country, and South African athletes, both men and women, were banned from taking part in international sporting events. Shunned by much of the world, South Africa became increasingly isolated.

Closer to home, too, South Africa was in trouble. Since the 1970s, the government had tried to dominate southern Africa, partly because some of South Africa's neighbors, such as Zambia, served as bases for ANC forces. In Angola, it supported the rebel UNITA movement, which was fighting the Soviet-backed government for control of the country. In 1988, Angola routed the South African troops that had invaded their country. The South African military's outdated weapons were no match for the Soviet arms used by the Angolans.

Mandela Is Freed

In September 1989, a new president, Frederik Willem de Klerk, replaced P.W. Botha. By now, many whites recognized that apartheid's days were numbered. The government began to release ANC leaders from prison, though not Mandela. Then at the opening session of parliament on February 2, 1990, de Klerk announced a dramatic change—the ban on the ANC and other protest groups was to be lifted. Nine days later Mandela walked free from prison, to the delight of millions around the world. He greeted the crowds that had gathered to celebrate his release with the word *"Amandla!"*—"Power!"—and they responded *"Ngawethu!"*—"To the people!"

In 1990–1991, the government finally abolished the apartheid laws, international sanctions were lifted, and the ANC suspended its armed struggle. The government began talks with the homelands,

A new ANC symbol, combining the flag and the spear and shield of the MK, was adopted in 1992.

ANC, and other political parties, with the aim of creating a free, democratic South Africa.

At times during the next two years, the discussions threatened to break down, and violence flared between the security forces, the ANC, and Buthelezi's Inkatha Freedom Party. In 1993, however, the negotiators succeeded in drafting a new constitution, and an election date was set for the following year.

First Democratic Elections

Between April 26 and April 29, 1994, voting took place in South Africa's first-ever democratic election. Long lines of Africans stood in the blazing sun for hours to cast their votes. When the results were announced, the ANC had won an overwhelming majority of seats in the National Assembly.

Residents of the black township of Katlehong, east of Johannesburg, stand in line to vote in the first all-race elections.

On May 9, the South African MPs (Members of Parliament) met to elect Nelson Mandela as South Africa's first black president, with de Klerk and Thabo Mbeki of the ANC as deputy presidents. The new constitution provided for a "Government of National Unity" for the next five years, until 1999. All parties with a significant number of seats could take part in government. The first "negotiated revolution"—the complete political restructuring of a nation with a minimum amount of violence—in history had been accomplished.

"One Law, One Nation"

South Africa's new constitution was adopted on May 8, 1996. The constitution begins with an introduction laying out the spirit governing the new nation. Here are its opening words:

We, the people of South Africa,

Recognize the injustices of our past;

Honor those who suffered for justice and freedom in our land;

Respect those who have worked to build and develop our country; and

Believe that South Africa belongs to all who live in it, united in our diversity.

For years, South Africa had been "the skunk of the world." In the 1970s, it had been banned from the United Nations (UN). Now it retook its seat at the UN and rejoined the British Commonwealth of Nations, after a gap of 33 years.

Building a New Country

At home, the apartheid regime had left enormous inequalities between black and white living standards. Whites enjoyed a better education, better medical care, superior housing, and greater job opportunities. The new government launched a major new program called the Reconstruction and Development Program (DRP). The program sought to improve housing and education, combat crime, and encourage economic growth.

In August 1994, Nelson Mandela gave a speech outlining the government's progress during its first 100 days in office. However, many people felt that the pace of change was not rapid enough, and after Mandela's speech, there were protests and industrial strikes.

In 1993, Nelson Mandela and F.W. De Klerk were jointly awarded the Nobel Peace Prize for their work in bringing about a multiracial South Africa.

Bill of Rights

The South African Bill of Rights is an important part of the country's Constitution and a cornerstone of its democracy. Some of its provisions are:

• "Everyone is equal before the law…"

• "Everyone has the right to life."

• "Everyone has the right to freedom and security…"

• "No one may be subjected to slavery…or forced labor."

• "Everyone has the right to freedom of conscience, religion, thought, belief and opinion."

• "No citizen may be deprived of citizenship."

SOUTH AFRICA'S ADMINISTRATION

Today, South Africa is a democratic republic. Every five years, everyone aged 18 and over can vote for candidates to represent them in the National Assembly. Collectively, the elected candidates—called Members of Parliament (MPs)—make the laws of the land and make sure that these laws serve the interests of the people. The MPs also elect the president, who, like the U.S. president, is both leader of the government and head of state. The president appoints a cabinet—the body that leads the government.

South Africa's nine provinces have considerable control over their own affairs. Each has its own local assembly, government, and premier, and each sends a delegation to parliament, made up of ten members including the premier. Together, the 90 provincial delegates make up the National Council of Provinces (NCP). The NCP can try to amend bills passed by the National Assembly before they are signed by the president and become law.

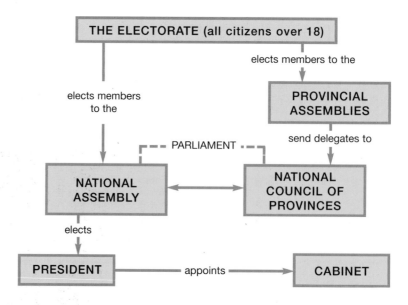

The South African political system resembles that of the United States, with two houses and a president who is both head of government and head of state.

THE SOUTH AFRICAN GOVERNMENT IN 2000

National Assembly (percentage of seats held by each party)
400 members • Last election 1999• Elections held every 5 years

ANC (African National Congress)	67%
DP (Democratic Party)	9.5%
IFP (Inkatha Freedom Party)	8.5%
NNP (New National Party)	7%
others	8%

National Council of Provinces
90 members • Formed by delegations from the provincial assemblies

ANC (African National Congress)	38%
DP (Democratic Party)	8%
New Komeito	8%
SDP (Social Democratic Party)	2%
others	44%

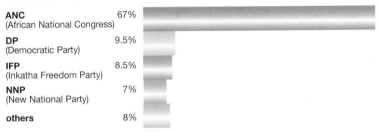

The African National Congress continues to dominate the National Assembly, with 266 of the total 400 seats. The Democratic Party, Inkatha, and the New National Party also have a strong presence in the assembly. The National Council of Provinces (NCP) is not an elected house and represents the interests of the provinces in Parliament. Each province, no matter how big or small, has ten seats in the NCP.

Political Parties

A large number of political parties are represented in the National Assembly and the National Council of Provinces. The African National Congress (ANC) is, however, by far the most popular political party and holds about two-thirds of the seats in the National Assembly. This also means that it runs South Africa's government.

There are three major opposition parties. The Democratic Party (DC) is supported by those whites who worry that their interests will be ignored in a fast-changing country. The Inkatha Freedom Party (IFP) represents mainly the interests of black Zulus in the province of KwaZulu-Natal. The old National Party, which long governed South Africa, has changed its name to the New National Party (NNP). Its main support is drawn from Afrikaners and other whites in South Africa.

The South African parliament is in Cape Town. The building below is the site of the National Council of Provinces (NCP).

The Economy

"A good head and a good heart are always a formidable combination."

South African president Nelson Mandela

In earlier times, both black and white inhabitants of what is today South Africa lived by farming and herding. However, with the discovery of rich reserves of gold and diamonds in the 19th century, mining quickly became the main source of the country's wealth and led to the development of factories and railroads. It was not long before South Africa became the leading industrial nation in Africa. Until the 1970s, South Africa's economy was able to grow by leaps and bounds, helped on its way by foreign investment.

During the 1980s, the economy slowed and foreign investors withdrew because of apartheid. The economic slowdown played a part in bringing apartheid to an end because businesspeople realized that the economy could not prosper unless South Africa was a part of the international community. Now that South Africa has become a democracy, foreign countries are beginning to invest in

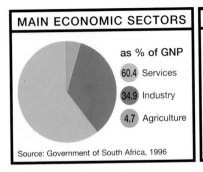

MAIN ECONOMIC SECTORS

as % of GNP

60.4 Services

34.9 Industry

4.7 Agriculture

Source: Government of South Africa, 1996

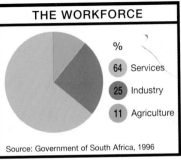

THE WORKFORCE

%

64 Services

25 Industry

11 Agriculture

Source: Government of South Africa, 1996

Almost all of South Africa's vineyards are found in the Western Cape, where the sunny, wet weather is favorable to the growth of good grapes.

the country again. Nevertheless, there are still huge differences between the incomes and living standards of the richest and poorest members of South African society.

MAJOR ECONOMIC SECTORS

Today, manufacturing is more important than mining in South Africa, generating around one-quarter of the total value of its goods and services each year. The largest economic area (or sector) in terms of employment is the service industry, which employs nearly two-thirds of the workforce. The service sector includes central and local government and social services. Other major sectors include farming, trade and finance, and tourism.

Ostrich farming begun in South Africa in around 1864. For more than 120 years, South Africa enjoyed a virtual monopoly on ostrich products, such as feathers and meats.

Crops and Livestock

Much of the land in South Africa is not suitable for farming. Some of the land is too high or too steep, while many parts of the country are too dry. Nevertheless, South Africa is usually able to grow enough food to feed itself and has a crop surplus, which it exports. South Africa accounts for one-fifth of all Africa's farm produce. The high plateau around Johannesburg is the largest arable (crop-growing) region in the country.

HOW SOUTH AFRICA USES ITS LAND

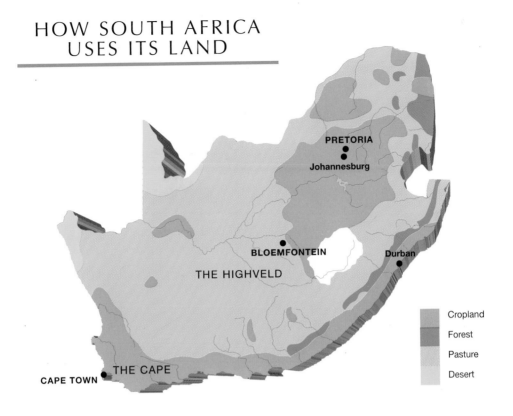

PRETORIA
Johannesburg
BLOEMFONTEIN
Durban
THE HIGHVELD
THE CAPE
CAPE TOWN

Cropland
Forest
Pasture
Desert

Two kinds of farming are practiced in South Africa: subsistence and commercial. Subsistence farmers use traditional organic methods and produce only enough crops to feed themselves and their families. Lately, the government has been helping small farmers to become more efficient and produce more crops. Commercial farms are large and, in South Africa, owned mainly by white people. Using modern fertilizers, they produce large quantities of crops to be sold locally or sent abroad.

Only 11 percent of South Africa—mostly the land along the coastal strips—is suitable for growing crops. The large areas of pasture found on the interior plateau are used for grazing.

Most of the western half of South Africa is too dry for farming. However, the grasslands of the Highveld provide good grazing for sheep and goats. Sheep were first brought to the country by white settlers in the 1650s. Today, wool is South Africa's main agricultural export. The climate of the south-

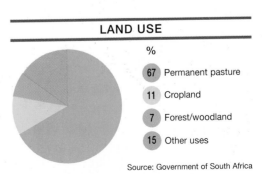

LAND USE

%

67 Permanent pasture

11 Cropland

7 Forest/woodland

15 Other uses

Source: Government of South Africa

South African Wines

In 1656, the first governor of the Cape Colony, Jan van Riebeeck (*see* p. 55), planted vines at the foot of Table Mountain. Three years later, wine was pressed from Cape grapes for the first time. Today, most South African wine is still produced in the Western Cape region. South African wines have been exported (sold outside the country) since the early 1900s. Between 1986 and 1991, however, these fresh, fruity wines became largely unavailable overseas owing to the economic sanctions imposed during apartheid. However, since the democratic elections of 1994 and the lifting of the sanctions, South African wines are again enjoying a large share of the world market.

western tip around Cape Town is wetter than other areas of the country. This is the main grape-growing region, famous for its fine wines (*see* box). Apples, wheat, and barley are also grown here.

In parts of the north and east, beef cattle are raised for meat. Dairy cattle, yielding milk and butter, graze the rich pastures around Port Elizabeth in the Eastern Cape and in the area around Pretoria in Gauteng. In hot and humid KwaZulu-Natal in the east, farmers grow citrus and tropical fruits, including oranges, pineapples, bananas, and mangoes. Sugarcane is grown on plantations along the east coast. South Africa is a major producer of the world's sugarcane.

Forestry and Fishing

Only a small portion of South Africa is covered by forest. In the 19th century, many trees were cut down for timber. Recent governments have encouraged a program of tree replanting, especially in the Great Escarpment, the mountainous area to the south and east of the country's vast interior plateau. Today, South Africa produces enough timber and wood pulp for its own needs, with some surplus left for export.

Given South Africa's long coastline, it is not surprising that fishing has become a major industry. About 90 percent of the catch comes from the cold Atlantic waters off the country's west coast. The government imposes tight controls over the numbers of fish that can be caught each year to prevent stocks from declining.

South Africa's national tree is the yellowwood tree, which can grow to a height of more than 130 feet (40 m).

The Mining Industry

To many people, South Africa is best known as a source of gold and diamonds. As the world's leading gold producer, South Africa mines over a third of the world's gold each year. The country also holds the world's largest stocks of chromium, platinum, vanadium, and manganese and is a major producer of coal, copper, diamonds, iron ore, nickel, antimony, and uranium. In total, some 60 different minerals are mined in South Africa.

The first South African gold was discovered in the Witwatersrand in 1886 (*see* p. 61). Within a few years, the buried riches had transformed the region, making a handful of mine-owners fabulously wealthy and even causing major wars. Gold is still the country's leading export, accounting for about half of the country's foreign earnings (the profit made from exports).

In the early days of mining, gold nuggets as large as 17.2 pounds (7.8 kg) were sometimes found near the surface. Today, this precious metal is not so easy to come by. It occurs in narrow bands of rocks called reefs, which are often found deep underground. South Africa's gold-bearing rocks lie in a great arc that stretches 300 miles (500 km) from Evander in Mpumalanga to Welkom in Free State. Johannesburg, the "city of gold," lies in the heart of the mining region. The ERPM (East Rand Proprietary Mines) mine nearby is one of the world's deepest. It is up to 3 miles (5 km) deep in places.

In South Africa, gold occurs in narrow veins, so large machines cannot be used to extract it. Instead, the rocks are removed by teams of miners with pneumatic drills. Below ground, the temperature rises

Most of South Africa's gold deposits are deep underground. This makes mining cramped and dangerous work. Mines can be up to 3 miles (5 km) deep.

Diamonds Are Forever

Diamond is the hardest naturally occurring substance known. It is a particularly pure form of the element carbon and can vary in appearance from colorless to black. In addition to being highly valued as gemstones, diamonds are also used in industry. Their renowned hardness makes them invaluable for cutting tough materials.

Diamonds are found in rocks called "pipes"—the vents of extinct volcanoes. Sometimes they are washed out of the pipes by streams and end up on riverbanks or on the seabed.

Rough, uncut diamonds look like pale pebbles and must be cut and polished before they shine and sparkle. The first diamonds at Kimberley were found at the surface. Later, the world's largest manually made hole, 787 feet (240 m) deep, was dug to extract them. In total, 33 million tons (30 million t) of earth were removed from the Big Hole (shown above) to mine 3.3 tons (3 t) of diamonds.

The Cullinan Diamond, found near Pretoria in 1905, was the largest diamond the world has ever known. Weighing 3,106 carats, it was presented to the British king Edward VII and cut into more than 100 gemstones. The largest, called the Star of Africa, was placed in the scepter of the British monarch. This pear-shaped gem weighs 530 carats and is the largest cut diamond in the world.

1.8°F (1°C) for every 300 feet (90 m) of descent. The deepest shafts are almost unbearably hot, and the air must be artificially cooled. The mined rock is crushed and ground into a pulp, then heated with cyanide to remove impurities before being poured into bars.

The gold-mining industry employs half a million workers, including thousands of South Africans, but also many laborers from neighboring countries. The miners have developed their own language, Fanakalo, a mix of Zulu, Afrikaans, and English words, so they can communicate with one other. Migrant workers live in hostels—shared, single-sex living quarters—near the mines and see little of their families from one year to the next. Recently, the government has begun taking steps to improve conditions for these workers.

Diamonds have been another source of enormous wealth (*see* box opposite). They were first discovered in 1866, near the Orange River. Then, in 1871, rich deposits were found at Kimberley. At first, many miners worked their own small claims at Kimberley, but within 20 years, the entire industry was controlled by Cecil Rhodes (1853–1902), owner of the wealthy De Beers Consolidated Mines. Rhodes also made a fortune from gold, owning Consolidated Mines in the Witwatersrand. Diamonds are still a major export, and South Africa is the world's fifth-largest diamond producer.

A Wealth of Coal

After gold, South Africa's next most valuable mineral, in terms of export earnings, is not diamond but coal. The country holds huge reserves of the fuel, enough to meet its own needs with large stocks left over for export. South Africa mostly exports to other African countries, supplying a remarkable 98 percent of the continent's coal.

Within South Africa itself, coal is burned in power plants to generate electricity. It is also made into synthetic (artificial) oil because oil is almost the only

In 1997, some 420 people lost their lives and 7,100 were injured in mining-related accidents in South Africa.

ENERGY SOURCES

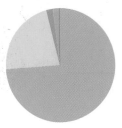

%

74 Coal

22 Oil

2 Gas

2 Nuclear

Source: Government of South Africa

South Africa's rich reserves of coal mean that the country relies heavily on the fuel to meet its energy needs. The relatively low cost of electricity produced using coal means that other, more energy-efficient technologies are not widely used.

South Africa covers only four percent of Africa, yet it provides more than half of the continent's electricity.

mineral in short supply. South Africa is a world leader in oil-from-coal conversion. Around 36 percent of the demand for liquid fuels is met by synthetic oil.

South Africa's main electricity company, Eskom, supplies power to many neighboring nations. Much of the electricity comes from coal-burning generating stations. Hydroelectric plants, gas turbines, and the nuclear power plant at Koeberg, near Cape Town, also generate electricity.

In 1992, only 40 percent of homes in South Africa had electricity. The new, nonracial government planned to bring power to 70 percent of households by 2000—a target it failed to meet. The country's industry is a big energy consumer. Despite having a GNP that ranks 26th in the world, South Africa's energy consumption is ranked 16th. This huge demand is largely created by the energy-intensive mining industries.

MAJOR INDUSTRIES

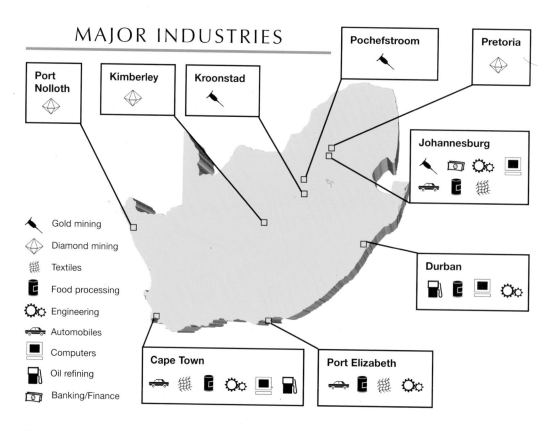

Port Nolloth

Kimberley

Kroonstad

Pochefstroom

Pretoria

Johannesburg

Durban

Cape Town

Port Elizabeth

Gold mining
Diamond mining
Textiles
Food processing
Engineering
Automobiles
Computers
Oil refining
Banking/Finance

Manufacturing

South Africa is the industrial giant of Africa, producing two-fifths of the continent's manufactured goods. In the late 19th century, the growth of the mining industry created a need for the development of manufacturing to supply the mines and equip the miners.

During the early 20th century, manufacturing grew quickly, fueled by abundant raw materials and cheap labor. In the 1940s, World War II provided a further boost to vehicle-manufacturers and other businesses. Today, manufacturing is South Africa's principal industry. The main industrial areas are the Johannesburg region, Cape Town, and the east coast, including the ports of Durban and Port Elizabeth.

South Africa is Africa's largest iron and steel producer. Iron ore, coke, and limestone are heated in blast furnaces and processed to make steel. The industry was originally developed to supply the gold and diamond mines with equipment. Now South African iron and steel are shipped to 80 different nations around the world.

Vehicle manufacture is another major industry. It, too, developed as a spin-off from mining because ships and trains were needed to transport ores and metals. Now South African automobiles, tractors, trucks, trains, ships, and planes are sold in many countries. Many vehicles are assembled in up-to-date factories where machines do much of the work.

Other major industries in South Africa include electronics, textiles, and food-processing. They produce goods ranging from bread to computers.

New Opportunities

Traditionally, South Africa's workforce was divided along ethnic lines. White people held all the skilled, well-paid jobs because they received better education and training. Black people did low-paid manual work; poor schooling, unjust laws, and racist attitudes barred them from senior jobs and banned them from even entering some professions. Now that apartheid has been abolished, South Africa is left with a shortage of skilled workers, particularly among blacks. The new government is working to correct this imbalance, and to provide better training and opportunities for nonwhites.

These tourists on safari have been lucky enough to catch sight of an elephant. The prospect of seeing some of the most astonishing animals in the world in their natural environment attracts many visitors to South Africa.

MAIN OVERSEAS ARRIVALS

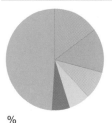

%

15 Swaziland

14 Zimbabwe

9 Botswana

7 Namibia

6 United Kingdom

49 Others

Source: Government of South Africa

Most overseas arrivals are still from African countries. However, the number of tourists from Europe and the United States is rising rapidly each year.

Tourism

Today, tourism is booming in South Africa. The injustices of the apartheid era made many people reluctant to visit the country. In the early 1990s, fewer than a million tourists visited every year. Now this figure is rising sharply, and because overseas visitors have to buy rands in order to buy goods and services, there are signs that tourism will soon overtake gold as South Africa's main foreign-currency earner. The tourist industry creates jobs for over a tenth of the workforce, including tour guides, park wardens, shopkeepers, craftspeople, drivers, and hotel and restaurant staff.

South Africa holds many attractions for tourists. Some people visit the country to enjoy the beautiful scenery or fine beaches or to see the spectacular wildlife in parks and reserves. Others come to pursue adventurous outdoor activities from hiking to bungee-jumping. Many tourists visit South Africa to find out more about the customs, way of life, and crafts of such peoples as the Zulu, Venda, and Ndebele. Ecotourism—visiting natural habitats without damaging them—is a fast-growing area, and many people now come to watch wildlife and photograph the landscape on trips that are designed not to damage the natural world.

MAIN TRADING PARTNERS

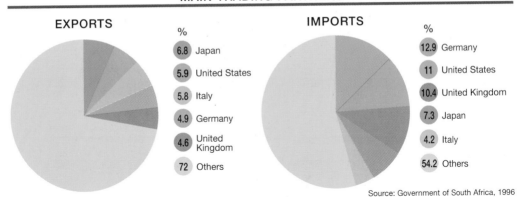

EXPORTS

%

6.8	Japan
5.9	United States
5.8	Italy
4.9	Germany
4.6	United Kingdom
72	Others

IMPORTS

%

12.9	Germany
11	United States
10.4	United Kingdom
7.3	Japan
4.2	Italy
54.2	Others

Source: Government of South Africa, 1996

Trade and Commerce

During the bleak days of apartheid, many countries refused to do business with South Africa. Now the new government has resumed trade with many nations. South Africa's main trading partners are the United States, Japan, and some European countries. The South African government is keen to encourage trade with other African nations. It aims to create an African economic union to promote Africa-wide economic and political unity and free trade.

Europe is South Africa's primary trading and investment partner and the chief source of finance and technology. South Africa's chief imports—machinery and equipment, vehicles, chemicals, petroleum, and manufactured goods—come mainly from Britain, Germany, the United States, and Japan. South Africa's chief exports are metals and minerals including gold, diamonds, and platinum, weapons, and farm produce, including wool, corn, sugar, and fruit. These goods go mainly to Japan, the United States, Italy, Germany, and the United Kingdom.

(Above) South Africa trades widely, but its principal trading partners are Japan, Germany, and the United States. (Below) South Africa typically has a trade surplus on its current account.

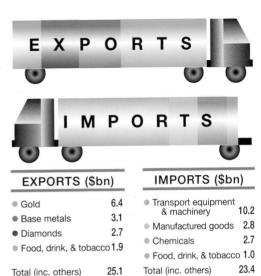

EXPORTS ($bn)	
● Gold	6.4
● Base metals	3.1
● Diamonds	2.7
● Food, drink, & tobacco	1.9
Total (inc. others)	25.1

IMPORTS ($bn)	
● Transport equipment & machinery	10.2
● Manufactured goods	2.8
● Chemicals	2.7
● Food, drink, & tobacco	1.0
Total (inc. others)	23.4

Source: Government of South Africa, 1996

At 21,000 miles
(34,000 km),
South Africa's
railroad network
is the ninth
longest in
the world.

TRANSPORTATION AND COMMUNICATIONS

South Africa's transportation network is the most efficient in Africa. A number of countries in southern
Africa use the South African transportation infrastruc-
ture to move their imports and exports.

The transportation system is run by a large, mainly
government-owned organization called Transnet. The
company is an important employer in South Africa, providing jobs for some 18,000 people. Different parts of
Transnet run the various transportation networks.
Spoornet runs the railroads, Autonet the roads; Portnet
makes sure that all the ports are running smoothly;
while South African Airways is the national airline.

On the Road

South Africa has a total of 91,000 miles (147,000 km)
of unpaved roads. In rural areas, most people travel on
foot or horseback, or ride in donkey carts. There are

TRANSPORTATION

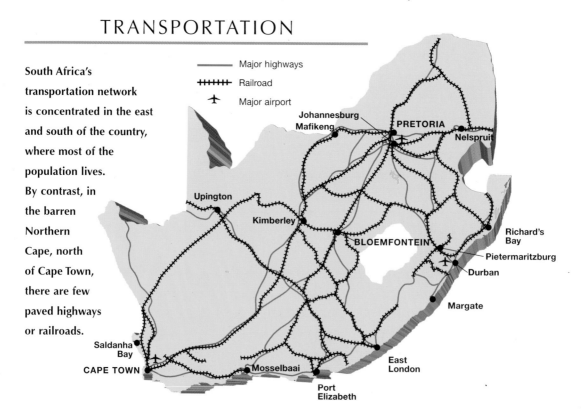

South Africa's
transportation network
is concentrated in the east
and south of the country,
where most of the
population lives.
By contrast, in
the barren
Northern
Cape, north
of Cape Town,
there are few
paved highways
or railroads.

Major highways

Railroad

Major airport

Johannesburg
Mafikeng
PRETORIA
Nelspruit

Upington

Kimberley

BLOEMFONTEIN

Richard's
Bay

Pietermaritzburg

Durban

Margate

Saldanha
Bay

CAPE TOWN
Mosselbaai
East
London

Port
Elizabeth

also more than 37,000 miles (60,000 km) of paved roads, mostly in well-populated areas. Highways link the major cities and connect South Africa with its neighbors.

Fast, long-distance buses are a familiar sight on these roads. Many people take a bus to visit their families on weekends. Within the cities, minibus taxis are a popular way to travel. These vehicles carry many passengers, and the drivers do not start until the buses are full. Competition between minibus drivers is fierce and occasionally escalates into violence. As a result, this form of travel can be dangerous. The new government is now taking steps to make minibus travel safer.

This colorful container port in Cape Town is one of six in South Africa. South African rivers are unnavigable so coastal shipping provides the only form of water transportation.

Taking the Train

Railroads are the lifelines of South Africa because most people do not own an automobile. Much of the railroad network was built in the early years of mining, when South Africa was part of the British empire. Now the nation has nearly 21,000 miles (34,000 km) of track. A remarkable 800 million passengers travel by train each year, and the network carries 220 million tons (200 million t) of freight annually. Every day, more than two million people leave their homes in the busy townships

The Blue Train

South Africa boasts one of the most luxurious trains in the world—the Blue Train. Originally known as the "Union Limited" on its journey from Johannesburg to Cape Town and as the "Union Express" on its return trip, the train got its present name owing to the distinctive sapphire-blue color of its carriages. The name stuck, and it was officially named the Blue Train in 1946.

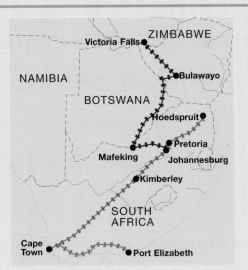

The train's predecessors were functional locomotives designed to transport miners to the diamond and gold mines near Johannesburg. The first luxury train was introduced in 1928 and has since been replaced twice, once in 1972 and again in 1997.

The current Blue Train runs between Pretoria and Victoria Falls, Hoedspruit, or Cape Town; and between Cape Town and Port Elizabeth. The most frequent journey made by the Blue Train is between Pretoria and Cape Town, three times a week. It is estimated that, in the next 25 years, the two new Blue Trains will cover 7.5 million miles (12 million km).

The modern Blue Train is primarily a tourist attraction, with 90 percent of its passengers coming from overseas. Travelers can enjoy private bathrooms, telephones, televisions, VCRs, and CD players. There are two lounges, one of which provides an engineer's-eye view of the track on a large screen.

and travel to city jobs by train. During the apartheid years, all trains had separate cars for black or white people. Third-class travel was reserved for blacks. Now anyone can sit in any part of the train.

South Africa's railroads are a great way to see the countryside. Magnificent steam trains run to many scenic destinations. The Blue Train is a world-famous luxury electric train that runs from Cape Town to Johannesburg and Pretoria (*see* box).

By Plane and Sea

South Africa has international airports at its three largest cities, Cape Town, Johannesburg, and Durban. Six more regional airports make travel inside the country quick and easy for those who can afford the fares. South African Airways carry around 45 million passengers each year.

The country has five major seaports—Cape Town, Durban, Port Elizabeth, Richards Bay, and Saldanha Bay, and one major river port, East London. All are well equipped to handle large quantities of freight.

Communications and Media

Both South Africa's mail and telephone services are run by publicly owned companies. Similarly, the government-owned South African Broadcasting Corporation controls most of the nation's radio and television. It operates nineteen radio services and three TV channels, which broadcast in nine languages, including Zulu, Xhosa, Hindi, English, and Afrikaans.

Half of the TV and radio programs broadcast are made in South Africa; the rest come from the United States, Britain, and elsewhere. There are also many independent radio stations, and subscription TV networks where viewers pay an annual or monthly fee to watch the available channels.

For many South Africans, the radio and TV are prize possessions. Radio, perhaps, has the greatest potential to reach a multicultural audience, and a total of 14 million people tune into a station each day. Television is also popular and attracts an audience of around 12 million a day.

Under apartheid, all books, films, and plays in South Africa were reviewed by the government's Publications Control Board. This organization was responsible for censoring or banning many works of a political nature that opposed apartheid. South Africa's new constitution guarantees freedom of speech, and the new government encourages free debate.

Telekom, the national telephone company, is responsible for 40 percent of all phone lines in Africa.

There are more than 30 daily and weekly newspapers in South Africa, most of which are written in English or Afrikaans. Only one newspaper qualifies as a national newspaper, however—the weekly *Mail & Guardian*.

Arts and Living

"I write what I like."

Title of a collection of Steve Biko's writings

South Africa is the meeting place of a great variety of cultures—black African, Dutch, British, Indian, and Malay. Yet, under the apartheid system, the racist white government suppressed or at best ignored almost every aspect of black, Asian, and colored ways of life. Conventional white lifestyles were the only kind recognized as having any value.

Apartheid laws tore many black families apart and forced black people to live outside the city downtown areas. Books and paintings that were critical of the regime were banned or censored, and black children were educated apart from white ones.

Black culture continued to flourish, however. Black musicians experimented with new, exhilarating styles; black churches offered comfort as well as inspiring gospel music; while antiapartheid rallies helped keep alive the traditions of black song and dance. In many cases, apartheid led both black and white people to write powerful novels, poems, or essays condemning the white regime and exposing the harsh realities of life in South Africa.

Today, after the end of apartheid, the government is working hard to create a truly multicultural society in South Africa. People of every color are free to mix and exchange ideas; galleries celebrate the work of long-banned black artists; and vibrant music festivals are attended by participants from all over Africa.

A Zulu woman threads beads to make a traditional beadwork belt. For many black South Africans, such crafts are an important link with their people's past.

FACT FILE

● At his inauguration as president, Nelson Mandela received the praises of an *imbongi*— a traditional black praise-singer.

● Under apartheid, the South African government banned *Black Beauty*— a children's book about a horse— on the grounds of its name alone.

● South Africa has a very high crime rate, with some 524 serious assaults per 100,000 of the population per year.

● Soccer is the most popular sport in South Africa— both in terms of spectators and players. The Soweto stadium holds 90,000 people.

THE ARTS

The arts in South Africa have a long, rich history. Traditions of painting, storytelling, music, and dance all stretch back hundreds, even thousands, of years. Since colonial times, Europeans, Asians, and other ethnic groups have added their own artistic traditions, and sometimes these have blended with African styles to make new forms.

During the apartheid era, many forms of art were used to protest against social injustice. Many artists and musicians were involved in the antiapartheid movement, and some were banned in South Africa. Others went into voluntary exile. Now that apartheid is over, the arts have taken on a new energy and beauty.

Painting and Sculpture

Painting in South Africa dates back many thousands of years, to the cave and rock art of the San people. Images of humans and animals are thought to have linked the San with their ancestors in the spirit world. Today, there are no living San artists in South Africa, but San rock art can be seen at about 3,000 sites around the country (*see* box opposite). The San also sometimes decorated ostrich eggshells, which they used as drinking vessels.

In the 17th century, Europeans introduced their own artistic traditions to the country. In colonial times, white artists often chose the South African landscape as their subject. Nineteenth-century artists, such as Thomas Baines and Frederick I'Ons, painted beautiful scenes of the country that also provide a historical record of South Africa at the time.

During the early 20th century, South African women artists, such as Irma Stern and Maggie Laubser, were influenced by

The Ndebele women of northeast South Africa paint the clay walls of their houses with bold, multicolored designs. Each Ndebele village often has its own design. This example comes from a village near Pretoria, Gauteng Province.

Rock Art

Southern Africa's earliest inhabitants, the San, lived in the caves of the Drakensberg Mountains. The San decorated some cave walls with depictions of animals and people that are full of energy and color. There are running hunters, armed with bows and spears; and there are giraffes, elephants, lions, antelopes, and other animals that the San found in their region. Experts think that the San painted these animals because they believed them to have special powers and not because they may have depended on them for food.

The oldest of the paintings that survive date back some 800 years. The most recent are from the 19th century, and they sometimes depict the white settlers with their horses and cattle. Earlier paintings must have faded. The pigments used by the San artists—red, yellow, brown, white, and ocher—are vulnerable to the weather.

experimental art movements in Europe. Lippy Lipshitz, Moses Kottler, and later Edoardo Villa were European sculptors who settled in South Africa and achieved international success.

In the 1930s, black artists from urban areas began to develop their own distinctive art styles. Many, such as Sfiso ka Mkame and Mslaba Dumile, depicted the life of black Africans in the townships. Their work and that of sculptors such as Sydney Kumalo helped to publicize the call for social change. In the new, democratic atmosphere of the 1990s, the work of many artists blended African and European styles. The beauty of nature has become a major theme for many artists once more.

Making Everyday Things Beautiful

Traditionally, black South Africans often decorated both their bodies and everyday objects. The Bantu-speaking peoples were skilled metal workers. They made objects out of gold, copper, and iron. These objects were an important part of their trade.

Today, pottery, basketware, and stone- and wood-carving are still important crafts for many black African peoples. The Ndebele of the Highveld are particularly skilled craftspeople. They decorate their pots and bowls with striking abstract patterns in bright colors.

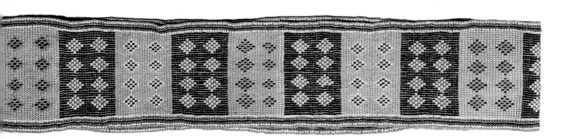

This intricately patterned beadwork neckband and belt were made by Zulu craftspeople. The belt—called an umbelenja—is worn by adolescent girls before marriage.

Beadwork is a centuries-old tradition among the Zulu, Xhosa, and Ndebele. The peoples of Southern Africa have traded for glass beads for generations, first with Arab peoples and later with Europeans. Both men and women wove beadwork headdresses, tunics, baskets, and jewelry. Bead designs

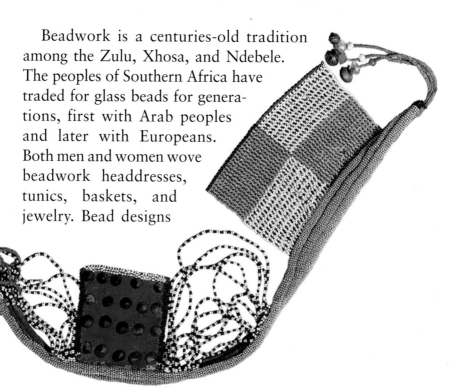

How to Say...in Zulu

The Zulu language is one of South Africa's 11 official languages and is the most widely spoken native language in South Africa. It is estimated that there are over six million people for whom Zulu is their mother tongue. The language has a big influence on the slang spoken by young people in cities.

Zulu belongs to the Nguni group of Bantu languages (*see* p. 53). As with some other Nguni languages, Zulu has borrowed the use of "clicking" noises from Khoisan—the language of the San and Khoikhoi. There are several kinds of click used. This makes it very hard for English-speakers to pronounce Zulu words properly without a lot of practice.

The Zulu people are very friendly, and there are lots of ways of greeting people or saying good-bye. Here are just a few examples of Zulu words:

Hello	*Sawubona*	Well, thank you	*Ngisaphila*
Good-bye (when leaving)		Please	*Jabulisa*
	Sala kahle	Thank you	*Ngiyabonga*
Good-bye (when staying)		Excuse me	*Uxolo*
	Hamba kahle	Yes	*Yebo*
How are you?	*Unjani?*	No	*Cha*

show the age and status of the wearer and the region the person comes from. Beads of different colors have various meanings—for example, white stands for love and purity, black for loneliness, and green for jealousy. Traditionally, the Zulu have used bead jewelry called *incwadi* to send messages to loved ones.

The Bantu peoples who today live in Northern Province are skilled wood carvers. The Venda decorate drums and doors with human figures and animals, while the Lovedu carve poles that are symbols of the power of their king or queen.

South Africa's native crafts are an important source of income for its black peoples, who sell their work to tourists. Because some carved objects have a sacred purpose, black sculptors who sell traditional works to white collectors are sometimes accused of betraying their people's secrets.

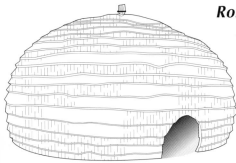

A Zulu hut (above)
is designed to create
a cool interior, away
from the summer
heat. The curved gables
and whitewashed walls
of this homestead
(below) are typical of
the Cape Dutch style.

Rondavels, Kraals, and Gables

South Africa is home to many styles of architecture. Traditional African dwellings are often made of adobe—sun-baked bricks of mud, dung, and straw—and topped with a thatched roof. One of the most common styles of house is the *rondavel*—a cylindrical house with a conical thatched roof. The design helps keep the interior of the hut cool in summer and warm in winter. By contrast, the traditional Zulu hut is shaped like a beehive.

Houses in native villages are often arranged in a circle, with a surrounding fence or wall, and with the cattle kept in a pen in the center. This kind of settlement is called a *kraal*. The Ndebele people decorate the walls of their houses with bright geometric patterns (*see* p. 98).

In the 17th century, Dutch settlers brought new building traditions to the country. During the 18th century, they developed their own style of architecture, called Cape Dutch. Their farmhouses and town buildings are decorated with curved

gables—the end-walls of a building near the roof—and ornate plasterwork. The most famous examples of Cape Dutch buildings are found in or near Cape Town.

Music—A Meeting of Traditions

South Africa has a very rich musical heritage. The traditional music of the San, South Africa's first native people, is mostly sung. Women sing choral (group) songs and clap their hands as an accompaniment to the ritual dances performed by men. San instruments are usually very simple. One of the most popular is the musical bow, which usually doubles as a hunting bow. The player holds the bow handle in his or her mouth and strikes the bow string with a small stick.

Bantu-speaking peoples, such as the Zulu and Xhosa, also sing choral songs. Dancers often sing as they dance, clapping their hands and shaking the rattles they wear about their ankles. Unlike many other African peoples, the Bantu rarely use drums to provide a rhythm for their dances. Individuals also make music, singing songs or playing simple instruments, such as a flute or musical bow.

Europeans, Asians, and other groups have all contributed their own styles to South African music (see box, for example). American music, too, is a strong influence. Gospel, rap, and reggae can be heard everywhere. During the 20th century, *mbaqanga*, or "township jive"—the music of the black townships—was very popular. It blended African tunes and rhythms with American jazz, rock, and blues. In the 1940s and 1950s,

Ghommaliedjie

One of the most vibrant musical traditions of South Africa is that of the Cape Muslims. Cape Muslim music dates back to the Malay slaves who were brought to South Africa in colonial times. These slaves were well-known for their musical talents and played for their Dutch masters at festivals and banquets. Their lively, witty songs were often accompanied by a small drum known as a *ghomma* and were called *ghommaliedjie* ("*ghomma* songs"). Modern Cape Muslim music incorporates Eastern, Western, and African influences and is accompanied by a guitar, cello, or *ghomma*.

kwela music, which features the sound of the penny whistle, was the first distinctively South African sound to become known abroad. Recently, the group Mango Groove won international fame playing *kwela* music.

The group Ladysmith Black Mambazo have a singing style based on traditional Zulu choral singing, known as *iscathamiya*. They shot to fame when they recorded the *Graceland* album with American singer Paul Simon. Among today's young people, though, the most popular music is *kwaito*—a rough-and-ready dance music, with lyrics sung in the ghetto slang known as *tsotsi-taal*.

Dance for All Occasions

Dance is important for the Zulu people. In the past, Zulu dances formed part of the preparations for war as well as more joyous ceremonies such as those accompanying marriage, birth, and coming of age.

Dance—like music—holds a special place in South African culture. Ceremonial dances accompany every stage of life, such as birth, coming of age, and marriage. Among the Venda people, for example, girls reaching puberty dance the *domba*, or python dance. Other dances were preparations for war or hunting.

In the apartheid years, dance was an important part of the black struggle against the government. Movements such as the Inkatha Freedom Party (IFP) and the United

Democratic Front, for example, used dance as a way of fostering solidarity. Such dances include the Conga-like *toyi-toyi* ("struggle dance of the people") and the *mapantsula*. Today, many styles of dancing flourish in South Africa, and dance groups include three major ballet companies.

Writing for Freedom

Literature has played an important role in South Africa for centuries, from oral story-telling to the written word. Among black African peoples, stories, myths, and praise poems (*see* box) have been passed down by word of mouth for generations. After the arrival of the Europeans, these spoken traditions were written down for the first time.

It was some time before white British and Afrikaner settlers wrote a literature about their own experience of life in South Africa. The first novel to treat the theme was Olive Schreiner's *Story of an African Farm* (1883), which tells of the hardships of farming on the Great Karoo. Adventure stories were also popular. The British emigrant H. Rider Haggard became famous for his novel *King Solomon's Mines* (1885).

In the 20th century, the injustices of apartheid inspired some of South Africa's best writing. White novelists such as Nadine Gordimer, André Brink, and Alan Paton wrote novels showing the damage inflicted on all peoples under apartheid. During the 1950s, the black magazine *Drum* launched the careers of many new black writers, including Lewis Nkosi and Mongane Wally Serote. Later, Steve Biko's powerful writings inspired black people everywhere to stand up to white oppression. Many political prisoners wrote harrowing accounts of their time in jail. Indres Naidoo, for example, wrote *Island in Chains*, an account of his ten years' stay on Robben Island.

Praise Poems

One of the most important forms of spoken art among the black peoples of South Africa is the praise poem, or *izibongo*. Traditionally, almost every young man tried his hand at creating and singing an *izibongo*, sometimes in praise of his cattle or even of himself. The singer was called an *imbongi*. A talented *imbongi* might be invited to sing in praise of a king or warrior. In the 20th century, praise poems are also performed at political meetings, in honor of the party leader.

In 1991, Nadine Gordimer became the only South African writer to have won a Nobel Prize in Literature.

The homes of wealthy whites in South Africa sometimes look more like fortresses than houses. This home in Johannesburg is surrounded by high walls, with cameras and electric fences. Crime rates in South Africa are soaring, and both blacks and whites live in fear of crime.

EVERYDAY LIFE

Even after the end of apartheid, the country's black and white populations live very different lifestyles. Most white people are well-off and live in comfortable, safe suburbs of the kind that are found throughout Europe and the United States. Most black people, by contrast, are very poor, and many live in crowded, crime-ridden, and unhealthy conditions.

Luxury and Squalor in the City

Living standards vary greatly in South Africa, both in town and country. During apartheid, most whites lived in prosperous suburbs. Many had luxury homes with swimming pools and employed black servants as gardeners, cooks, and cleaners.

Statistics on South Africans' standards of living are hard to come by. Those statistics that are available conceal the big gap in wealth that exists between black and white.

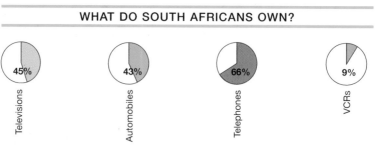

WHAT DO SOUTH AFRICANS OWN?

45% Televisions

43% Automobiles

66% Telephones

9% VCRs

Source: Government of South Africa; charts show percentage of households owning goods

Under apartheid, black people were not allowed to live in any city downtown. Instead, they lived in townships miles beyond the suburbs and faced a long journey to work each day. Now apartheid laws have been abolished, but most blacks still live in low-standard housing. In the mid-1990s, the government estimated that up to 20 million people were without adequate sanitation and electricity. They also found that some eight million people lived in shantytowns—ramshackle settlements built of corrugated iron, driftwood, and plastic.

In 1994, as part of the Reconstruction and Development Program (RDP), the government started to tackle the housing crisis. It promised to build 30,000 new homes each year for the next ten years, but such improvements happen only slowly. Townships and camps still have few facilities, such as parks, clinics, schools, and community centers.

There are few supermarkets, so people buy food and essentials from markets and from backstreet stores called *spazas*. At night, many *spazas* double as unlicensed drinking houses called *shebeens*. In the past, apartheid governments saw the *shebeens* as a threat to law and order because they often served as a meeting place for discontented black youth.

Unemployment

In both town and countryside, high unemployment is a big problem, particularly among black people. In the mid-1990s, the government estimated that as many as ten million people were out of work, nearly a quarter of the population. The government is trying to solve this problem by providing work for builders, electricians, and plumbers, and also for teachers and medical staff. One difficulty is the very high proportion of black people who lack skills and training. New initiatives provide nonwhites with the skills they need to find employment.

In the Countryside

There is also a great gulf between black and white living standards in the countryside. White farmers own almost all of the arable (crop-growing) land, since the apartheid system forced many black farmers to give up their small-

A black woman bathes her child in a tub in the township of Soweto. Running water is quite rare in township homes, and people often have to collect their water from a pipe in the street.

Some 15 percent of South Africans do not have any schooling.

ATTENDANCE AT SCHOOL

College/university 3.1%

High school 23.5%

Elementary 85.1%

holdings (small farms). During the apartheid years, black South Africans were forced either to live in reserves—the "homelands"—or move to factory hostels or townships (*see* pp. 42–43) serving mines and cities. Post-apartheid governments are working to improve this situation, redistributing land and improving conditions in hostels.

Many homes in country areas lack clean water, sewage disposal, and electricity. In villages, mudbrick houses thatched with straw are often grouped around a meeting place or cattle pen. Conditions are cramped in the houses of black Africans both in the town and country because homes often contain extended families. Parents, children, grandparents, and often other relatives and their children, all live together under one roof. The new government is working to improve rural living standards, building new homes, putting up power lines, and sinking wells.

Schooling for All

In the past, the government spent far more on education for whites than for blacks, with the result that black schools were ill-equipped and had far fewer teachers. In black schools during the 1980s, classes of 50 pupils or even more were common. White classes contained only about 20 pupils on average. During the early 1990s, research showed that almost all white people were literate —that is, able to read and write. By contrast, only 75 percent of coloreds and 50 percent of blacks were literate.

Education is a priority for the new government. It aims to provide ten years of free schooling for all children, up to the age of about 15. In January 1995, it became compulsory for all children to attend school. Black pupils receive lessons in their own languages but also in English and Afrikaans so they can continue their studies at higher levels.

The government has also launched an adult education program to help the so-called "lost generation" of South Africans whose schooling was disrupted by the turbulent apartheid years. To meet all of the government's targets in education, many new schools and colleges are being built.

Traditionally, South Africa's higher education system was also divided along racial lines. Eleven universities were reserved for white students, with three for blacks, and one each for Asians and people of mixed race. Now all of these institutions are open to everyone.

How to Say...in Afrikaans

Afrikaans is not only the first language of the Boers, or Afrikaners; it is also spoken by many Asian and colored peoples, including the Cape Muslims. Afrikaans developed from Dutch, the language of South Africa's first colonial settlers, but it also includes words from English and French, as well as African and Asian languages. It is one of South Africa's official languages. Try out these few Afrikaans phrases; the letters in the parentheses show how the words should be pronounced.

Yes	*Ja* (yah)	Please	*Asseblief* (uhssehbleef)
No	*Nee* (ni)	Thank you	*Dankie* (dankee)
Hello	*Hallo* (hallo)	How are you?	*Hoe gaan dit?* (hoyeh gun dit)
Good morning	*Goeiemere* (geemorreh)	Well, thank you	*Goed dankie* (goot)

South Africa has one of the world's highest incidences of tuberculosis (TB), with some 205 cases for every 100,000 people.

Back to Health

In the past, black and white South Africans received very uneven standards of health care. Nonwhites had poorer care and ate a less varied diet. The result was that by the 1990s, white people could expect to live to the age of 73 on average, while the life expectancy for nonwhites was 63. Post-apartheid governments have pledged to raise general standards of medical care. Today, many new doctors and nurses are being trained, and new hospitals and clinics are being built.

South Africa remains a country full of contrasts in medical practice. On the one hand, the nation has a proud history of pioneering medicine. For example, in 1967, the Cape Town surgeon Christiaan Barnard carried out the world's first-ever heart transplant operation. On the other hand, a great many black citizens look to traditional African medicine to cure their ailments. Traditional healers follow various methods. Some interpret omens or other signs to diagnose sickness. Others use the healing properties of plants.

In the past, there has been little common ground between traditional African and Western medicine. However, the new government now recognizes all traditional healers as health workers.

The Manyanos

Women played little part in South Africa's native black religions. Christianity gave many black women their first chance to have a spiritual life. At the end of the 19th century, black Christian women began to form prayer groups, called *manyanos*. There the women could pray, preach, and draw strength and comfort from each other's company. Each group developed its own uniform and often played an important role in local communities, especially during the hard apartheid years. During this time, some people criticized the *manyanos* for their nonpolitical stance. The *manyanos* still remain at the heart of black South African women's spiritual life.

Religion

Religion plays an important part in everyday life in South Africa, and most people attend church regularly. Most churches hold evening meetings as well as Sunday services, and many people go along to worship and meet with their friends.

These women belong to the Church of Zion—South Africa's largest independent church. Members wear distinctive clothes, including a badge featuring a silver star on a green background.

Around 68 percent of South Africa's population are Christian. The most popular faith is the Dutch Reformed church, which has many Afrikaner and colored members. Many English-speakers belong to the Roman Catholic, Methodist, Anglican, Presbyterian, or Baptist churches. Of these, the Anglican church has the biggest role in South African society, in part thanks to its exuberant black archbishop, Desmond Tutu (born 1931; *see* p. 118), who spent many years campaigning for black rights.

Many other people are either Muslims, Hindus, or Jews. About one in ten follow traditional African religions and revere the spirits of their ancestors. Fifteen percent of all South Africans belong to independent Christian churches such as the Zion Christian church. These faiths combine elements from both Christianity and African religions.

Sports and Leisure

With sunny skies and a mild climate, South Africa is an ideal country for outdoor sports. Many people spend much of their free time in the open air, either watching sports or playing it themselves. During the apartheid era, many countries banned South Africa's national

As a nation, South Africans spend most of their money on food and drink.

HOW SOUTH AFRICANS SPEND THEIR MONEY

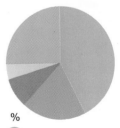

%

35 Food/drink

20 Housing/ household goods

15 Transportation

7.5 Clothing

22.5 Other

Source: Government of South Africa

Rugby Union

Rugby Union is a football game played throughout the world. It was first developed in Britain in the 1800s. According to legend, it was invented when a student at the prestigious Rugby School in England broke soccer rules by picking up the ball and running with it. The game quickly spread across the British empire, and today it is still popular in former British colonies, such as Australia, New Zealand, and South Africa.

Rugby is a very tough and fast-moving game. Two teams of 15 players compete for possession of an oval ball. A player scores a "try" by touching the ball down in the opposing team's goal area. Having scored a try, the scoring team also gets a chance to kick for extra points. If the kicker succeeds, his team gets more points, similar to a field goal in American football.

Rugby Union was first played in South Africa in the late 19th century. As in Britain, it was considered an elitist sport, played mainly by whites and especially by Afrikaners. There were a few black players, particularly in the Eastern Cape. Generally, though, blacks associated the game with the racist white regime.

The national team is the Springboks. Under apartheid, all the players in the national team were white. In 1995, however, a black player named Chester Williams was able to represent his country in the Rugby World Cup, held in South Africa. There were great celebrations when Williams scored the winning try in the final and President Mandela presented the cup to the captain. Here the Springboks—wearing their team colors of green and yellow—are competing against France in 1998.

National Holidays

Many of South Africa's national holidays celebrate the end of apartheid and the values of the new government.

January 1	New Year's Day	June 16	Youth Day
March 21	Human Rights Day	August 9	National Women's Day
March/April	Good Friday	September 24	Heritage Day
March/April	Easter Monday	December 16	Day of Reconciliation
April 27	Freedom Day	December 25	Christmas Day
May 1	Workers' Day	December 26	Day of Goodwill

teams from taking part in international sporting events, as part of the boycott against the country (*see* p. 75). Since 1991, when the boycott was lifted, South African teams have competed on the international scene again.

Soccer is the most popular sport in South Africa, particularly among black people. There are 15,000 clubs, with nearly a million players among them. Thousands of supporters pack large stadiums such as Soccer City near Johannesburg to watch their favorite teams in action. Soweto teams, such as Kaizer Chiefs and Orlando Pirates, draw big crowds. Rugby Union is another much-loved sport (*see* box opposite).

Cricket and golf are also national passions. There are major cricket fields at Port Elizabeth, Cape Town, and Johannesburg. For golfers, the beautiful grounds of the Lost City hotel complex in North-West Province are the setting for South Africa's leading tournament, the Sun City Million Dollar Challenge.

Boxing is also popular among both black and white people. Many young boys spend their free time sparring in the gym or training on open ground. Great boxing heroes include Dingaan Thobela ("the Rose of Soweto"), Welcome Noita, and Brian Mitchell.

In track events, South Africans excel in both sprint and long-distance running. One of the top races is the Comrades Marathon, which covers a distance of 55 miles

In 1996, South Africa's national soccer team won the African Nations Cup. In 1998, it also qualified for the first time for the World Cup.

(88 km) between Durban and Pietermaritzburg. The marathon started 40 years ago as a race between friends; now 14,000 runners take part and thousands of spectators line the route.

Tennis, netball (similar to six-player girls' basketball), and cycling are also favorite sports in South Africa. In the vacation season, the Drakensberg, Cedarberg, and other mountain ranges attract climbers, hikers, pony-trekkers, and hang gliders. Some people on vacation visit the rivers for trout fishing, canoeing, or white-water rafting. Many others head for the coast to enjoy watersports such as surfing, scuba diving, waterskiing, and sailing.

Food and Drink

The food in South Africa is as varied as its people. Settlers from many nations have contributed their dishes and cooking styles. Dutch and German immigrants brought cakes and tasty meat dishes. Protestants from France added wine recipes, tarts, and *konfyt*—fruit preserves. Hot curries and samosas are the mainstays of Indian cooking. Malays and other East Asian peoples added sweet and sour flavors and spicy pickles. The British brought a love of roasted meats and heavy desserts. Greek, Chinese, Portuguese, and American cooking are also enjoyed.

Many South African dishes feature meat and local game, including beef, lamb, springbok, wild boar, and ostrich. Because meat does not stay fresh long in hot weather, it is traditionally dried and cut into strips called *biltong*, which make a nourishing snack. In warm weather, South Africans like nothing better than a *braai*—an outdoor barbecue. The delicious smell of sizzling meat wafts across the suburbs, as steaks, kebabs, and *boerewors* (spicy sausages) cook in the open air. When the *braaivleis* (grilled meats) are done,

A Zulu woman prepares a traditional drink at Shakaland, a re-creation of a traditional Zulu village in KwaZulu-Natal.

South African Melktert

One of South Africa's most famous desserts is *melktert* ("milk tart")—a delicious, egg-custard tart first cooked by Afrikaners but today enjoyed by almost everyone. For this recipe, get an adult to make the pastry base for the tart, while you make the filling.

You will need: a baked 9-inch (23-cm) tart shell, 2 ounces (50 g) sugar, 1 tablespoon cornflour, 1 pint (575 ml) milk, stick of cinnamon, 10 ounces (25 g) butter, 2 beaten eggs, a few drops of vanilla extract.

Method: Begin by combining the sugar, cornflour, and a little of the milk to make a smooth paste. Pour the remaining milk into a saucepan. Add the cinnamon stick and bring the milk gently to a boil. Mix a little of the milk into the cornflour mixture, add this to the pan. Keep on heating the milk, stirring for about a minute. Remove the cinnamon, stir in the butter, and then take the pan off the fire. Leave the milk to cool.

Once the milk mixture is cool, beat in the eggs and vanilla extract. Pour the mixture carefully into the cooked pastry shell. Get an adult to bake the tart in the oven at 350°F (180°C) for about 40 minutes, then leave to cool. Enjoy!

they are eaten with salads and washed down with beer or wine. Fish and shellfish also feature in many recipes. National favorites include rock lobster and a succulent ocean fish called *snoek*.

Traditional African cooking is much simpler, yet still nourishing. The staple food of the townships and villages is cornmeal, or "mealies," ground and cooked into a porridge known as "pap." Many families eat pap at every meal, sometimes with vegetables such as pumpkin, sweet potato, and greens, and less often, with stewed meat or broth. More unusual African foods include fried mopani worms and eleven species of edible insects.

Local wines are popular in South Africa. The nation's vineyards produce both red and white varieties. A grasslike plant called sorghum is brewed to make a kind of beer. Tea is the most popular hot drink.

The Future

"In time, we shall be in a position to bestow on South Africa the greatest possible gift: a more human face."

Twentieth-century black activist Steve Biko

In April 1994, South Africa experienced radical political change when it achieved democracy. After election day was over, however, people realized that very little had actually changed in everyday life. Whites still owned almost all the country's wealth and money, and held the reins of business. Most black people remained poor, ill-housed, and unskilled, and many were out of work. Around the world, South Africa's transformation was hailed as a miracle. But it soon became clear that more miracles were needed if the country was to become a more just place.

The tasks facing the new government were tremendous. It had to attempt nothing less than the entire reorganization of society, to move toward a fairer distribution of power, land, and wealth. At the same time, it had to carry out its election promises to tackle poverty and unemployment, improve health care and education, and raise living standards.

THE SLOW PACE OF CHANGE

During the late 1990s, South Africa achieved progress in all these areas, but change did not always come as quickly as many had hoped. Unemployment remained a problem. The Reconstruction and Development Program (RDP) provided jobs and training for many workers, but South Africa's rising population meant

South Africa's best hope lies with its children. Now that all children are educated together, South Africa can become a truly multicultural nation.

117

that millions were still without a job. Similarly, in its first term of office, the government built thousands of new homes, particularly in urban areas. At the same time, however, thousands of people moved from country to urban areas in search of work and a better life. The cities were still full of people without proper homes, with millions living in tumbledown shacks.

TRUTH AND RECONCILIATION

To help achieve peace in South Africa's multicultural society and to deal with the accusations of crimes committed during apartheid, the government set up a pioneering committee called the Truth and Reconciliation Commission (TRC). It was chaired by the Anglican archbishop Desmond Tutu, a veteran civil-rights campaigner and Nobel Prizewinner.

Starting in 1996, the commission heard statements from hundreds of victims, awarded compensation, and offered amnesty (pardon) to those who confessed their crimes. After several months of hearings, it found the previous white government guilty of many crimes, including killings, torture, and abduction. It also criticized the ANC and the Inkatha Freedom Party (IFP) for violent acts.

In the years following the end of apartheid, the new South Africa has also experienced other threats to unity and stability. Several political organizations seek greater

Members of the Truth and Reconciliation Commission (TRC) face questions from the media. The white South African on the left is Alex Borraine, the MP for Cape Town, and next to him is Archbishop Desmond Tutu, head of the Anglican church in South Africa. The committee and the nation as a whole face an important moral question: How far should a country be prepared to forgive the crimes of the past for the sake of a harmonious future?

self-rule or independence from the state. The Zulu-dominated IFP wants more autonomy for the provinces, particularly the homeland of KwaZulu-Natal, which it controls. The right-wing Freedom Front, an organization of Afrikaners, demands a *volkstaat* ("people's state"), a separate, white-run state.

In 1996, Nelson Mandela announced that he would retire before the 1999 election, and nominated deputy president Thabo Mbeki (*see* box) to take his place. In 1997, he stepped down as leader of the ANC and was replaced by Mbeki. In South Africa itself, and internationally, millions regard Mandela as a great hero. At least in part, they attribute the country's smooth transition to democracy to his great statesmanship and charisma. Thabo Mbeki faces a daunting prospect in following Mandela.

Thabo Mbeki

South Africa's new president, Thabo Mbeki (born 1942), represents a younger generation of the black struggle against apartheid than Nelson Mandela. During the 1960s, while in exile, Mbeki was involved in developing the youth and student sections of the ANC. Later, in the 1980s, he worked with the international media to strengthen opposition to apartheid. After his return from exile in 1990, he became first the chairperson of the ANC and, in 1994, deputy president of the Republic of South Africa.

A NEW BEGINNING?

The government faces enormous challenges, but the mood of the country is mainly upbeat. The vast majority of South Africans are united in their desire for peace and progress. In economic terms, South Africa is the strongest country in Africa. The nation's mineral wealth, well-developed industry, and good communications mean there is great potential for further economic growth.

South Africa is on its way to becoming a leading democratic nation and may be a force for positive change in Africa as a whole. The main challenge facing post-apartheid governments is to make sure the country's prosperity is shared by the majority of its citizens, not just a fortunate few.

Almanac

POLITICAL

Country name:
Official form: Republic of South
  Africa
Short form: South Africa

Nationality:
 noun: South African
 adjective: South African

Official languages: Afrikaans, English,
 Ndebele, Pedi, SeSotho, Swazi,
 Tsonga, Tswana, Venda, Xhosa,
 Zulu

Capital cities:
 Pretoria (administrative),
 Cape Town (legislative),
 Bloemfontein (judicial)

Type of government:
 democratic republic

Suffrage (voting rights):
 everyone 18 years and over

Independence: May 31, 1910

National anthem:
 Combination of "Die stem
 van Suid-Afrika" and
 "Nkosi Sikelel"

National holiday:
 April 27 (Freedom Day)
Flag:

GEOGRAPHICAL

Location: The southern tip of the
 continent of Africa; latitudes
 22° to 35° south and
 longitudes 17° to 32° west

Climate: Mostly semiarid;
 subtropical along east coast

Total area: 471,445 square miles
 (1,221,043 sq. km)
 land: 100%
 water: 0%

Coastline: 1,739 miles (2,798 km)

Terrain: An interior plateau
 surrounded by rugged hills
 and a coastal plain

Highest point: Njesuthi
 11,181 feet (3,408 m)

Lowest point: Atlantic Ocean
 0 feet (0 m)

Land use (1993 est.):
  forests and woodland: 7%
  arable land: 11%
  permanent pastures: 67%
  other: 15%

Natural resources: tin, gold, copper,
  iron ore, coal, gas, uranium, gem
  diamonds, platinum, chromium,
  manganese

Natural hazards: droughts

POPULATION

Population (2000 est.): 43,982,000

Population growth rate (1999 est.):
  1.3%

Birthrate (1999 est.): 26 births
  per 1,000 of the population

Death rate (1999 est.): 13 deaths
  per 1,000 of the population

Sex ratio (1999 est.): 98 males per
  100 females

Infant mortality rate (1999 est.):
  52 deaths per 1,000 live births

Life expectancy at birth (1999 est.):
  total population: 54.76 years
  male: 52.68 years
  female: 56.9 years

Literacy:
  total population: 81.8%
  male: 81.9%
  female: 81.7%

ECONOMY

Currency: rand (R); 1 rand = 100 cents

Exchange rate (1998):
  $1 = R5.86

Gross national product (1996):
  $130.2 billion

Gross national product by sectors:
  agriculture: 4.7%
  industry: 34.9%
  service: 60.4%

GNP per capita (1998 est.): $6,800

Average annual inflation rate
  (1990–1998): 9.9%

Unemployment rate (1998): 30%

Exports (1996): $25.1 billion
Imports (1996): $23.4 billion

Foreign aid received: $497 million

Human Development Index
(an index scaled from 0 to 100 combining statistics
indicating adult literacy, years of schooling, life
expectancy, and income levels):
  71.7 (U.S. 94.2)

TIME LINE—SOUTH AFRICA

World History

South African History

c. 5,000,000 B.C.

c. **4,000,000** Hominids first develop in eastern and southern Africa.

c. 1,000,000 B.C.

c. **1,000,000** *Homo erectus* becomes the dominant species of hominid.

c. 50,000 B.C.

c. **40,000** Modern humans—*Homo sapiens sapiens*—emerge.

c. **30,000** The San peoples roam over Southern Africa.

c. A.D. 100

98–117 Roman empire reaches its greatest extent.

c. **200** Great Zimbabwe first settled by Iron Age people.

c. **100** The arrival of Nguni-speaking peoples force the San and Khoikhoi to move to lands in the west and southwest.

1837 Queen Victoria ascends the throne of Britain.

1834 Britain oulaws slavery

1815 French Emperor Napoleon is defeated at Waterloo.

1807 Britain outlaws the slave trade.

European countries set up colonies throughout Africa.

1648 Formation of the Dutch Republic.

1619 Europeans import the first slaves into Virgina.

1492 Christopher Columbus arrives in America—Europe begins period of global exploration and colonization.

1836 The Great Trek: Boers begin to leave Cape Colony and seek new farmlands in the interior.

1814 Cape Colony becomes part of the British empire.

c. **1800** The Difaqane forces thousands of Africans to flee inland as a new Zulu kingdom is established in the east.

c. 1800

1652 First Dutch settlers arrive at the site of Cape Town, led by Jan van Riebeeck.

c. 1600

1488 Portuguese navigator Bartholomeu Dias rounds the Cape of Good Hope.

c. 1400

c. 1850

1858 Britain takes direct responsibility for India

1861–1865 American Civil War.

1882 Britain occupies Egypt.

1891 Germany occupies Tanzania (German East Africa).

1852–1854 Foundation of the Boer Republics: The Transvaal and the Orange Free State.

1879 The British defeat the Zulu in the Anglo-Zulu War.

1880–1881 The Boers defeat the British in the First Anglo-Boer War.

1899–1902 The British defeat the Boers in the South African War.

2000 The West celebrates the Millennium—2,000 years since the birth of Christ.

1999 Thabo Mbeki replaces Mandela as president.

c. 1995

1994 First democratic elections are held. Mandela becomes the country's first black president.

1990 Nelson Mandela is released from prison after 28 years.

1989 Under pressure, F.W. de Klerk becomes president; he begins to dismantle apartheid.

c. 1900

1914–1918 World War I

1929 The Great Depression

1931 Britain establishes the Commonwealth of Nations.

1939–1945 World War II

1947 India becomes an independent nation.

1910 The Union of South Africa is formed; Louis Botha becomes its first prime minister.

1912 Foundation of the African National Congress.

1948 First all-Afrikaner government of South Africa is elected; the foundations of apartheid are laid down.

1993 Bill Clinton becomes U.S. President.

1989 Communism collapses in eastern Europe.

1986 The European Community and the United States impose economic sanctions on South Africa.

c. 1980

1980 Britain recognizes the independence of its last African colony, Rhodesia.

1969 The first human lands on the moon.

1963–1975 The Vietnam War

1961 South Africa becomes a republic and leaves the Commonwealth of Nations.

1960 The army kills 69 black people in the Sharpeville Massacre.

c. 1950

Glossary

Abbreviation:
Af. = Afrikaans
Du. = Dutch (Old)
Zu. = Zulu

Afrikaans: A language spoken by Afrikaners; developing from Dutch.

Afrikaner (Du. "African"): A white South African descended from the Dutch settlers.

ANC (African National Congress): A black political organization that fought against white rule in South Africa; today, as a political party, it holds the majority of seats in the South African parliament.

apartheid (Af. "separateness"): The system enforced by the white government of South Africa from 1948 to 1994, whereby people of different races were kept apart.

Bantu: A branch of the Niger-Kordofanian family of African languages.

bantustans (Af.): Lands reserved for black people under apartheid.

Boer (Du. "farmer"): Dutch settler who farmed land in South Africa.

boycott: A refusal to trade or have dealings with a company or country, usually as part of a moral protest.

Cape Dutch: A style of architecture developed by Dutch settlers in the 18th century.

colony: A territory owned by another country.

colored: In South Africa, a person of mixed race.

Commonwealth: A group of independent countries that share an allegiance to the British Crown.

constitution: The fundamental principles that underlie the government of a country.

democracy: A process that allows all the people of a country to govern themselves, usually by voting for a leader or leaders.

Difaqane: The forced migration inland of African tribes as a result of the expansion of the Zulu empire in the 1820s; sometimes called Mfecane.

discrimination: The act of treating people differently on the basis of race, sex, or other grounds.

empire: Extent of overseas territories owned or ruled by a country.

exports: Goods sold by one country to another.

Great Trek, the: The journey made by thousands of Boers to settle new land in the north and east of South Africa.

gross national product (GNP): Total value of goods and services produced by the people of a country during a period, usually a year.

guerrillas: Nongovernment fighters with political aims; avoiding direct conflict, they may use sabotage, raids, or ambushes as part of their campaign.

impis (Zu.): Units of highly trained Zulu soldiers in the 19th century.

imports: Goods bought by one country from another.

independence: The freedom of a nation or people from the rule of another nation.

industrial nation: A country where manufacture is usually carried out with the help of machinery.

Khoisan: One of the two African language families spoken in South Africa; characterized by a distinctive clicking sound that appears before most words.

kraals: Settlements where Nguni-speaking groups of Africans lived.

literacy: The ability to read and write.

massacre: The killing of a large number of usually defenseless people.

multicultural/multiracial: A society where different cultures and races live peacefully together and diversity is celebrated.

natural resources:
Minerals and other natural phenomena that can be harnassed to provide energy or raw materials for manufacture.

Nguni: A group of Bantu languages spoken in South Africa; examples include Zulu, Xhosa, and SeSotho.

nomadic: Term used to describe a lifestyle that involves migration from place to place in search of food or shelter.

sanctions: An agreement by several countries to economically isolate another country by refusing to trade with it.

savannah: Tropical grassland dotted with trees and bushes.

subtropical: A climate zone that borders on the tropical (between the Tropics of Cancer and Capricorn); subtropical regions are generally hot with periods of heavy rainfall.

township: An urban area on the outskirts of major cities, such as Johannesburg, built during apartheid to house nonwhite South Africans.

veld (**Du.** "field"): Areas of high-lying grassland on South Africa's interior plateau.

voortrekkers (**Af.** "pioneers"): Those Boers who went on the Great Trek.

Bibliography

Major Sources Used for This Book
Barber, J. *South Africa in the Twentieth Century.* Oxford, U.K.: Blackwell, 1999.

Laband, J. *The Rise and Fall of the Zulu Nation.* London, U.K.: Cassell Military, 1998.

Ross, R. *A Concise History of South Africa.* Cambridge, U.K.: Cambridge University Press, 1999.

General Further Reading
Clawson, E. *Activities and Investigations in Economics.* Reading, MA: Addison-Wesley, 1994.

Martell, H.M. *The Kingfisher Book of the Ancient World.* New York: Kingfisher, 1995.

The DK Geography of the World. New York: Dorling Kindersley, 1996.

The Kingfisher History Encyclopedia. New York: Kingfisher, 1999.

Student Atlas. New York: Dorling Kindersley, 1998.

Taborelli, G. *Art: A World History.* New York: Dorling Kindersley, 1998.

Further Reading About South Africa
Bradley, C. *Causes and Consequences of the End of Apartheid.* Causes and Consequences. Austin, TX: Raintree Steck-Vaughn, 1995.

Finlayson, R. *Nelson Mandela.* A&E Biographies. Minneapolis, MN: Lerner, 1998.

McSharry, P., H. Lewin, and R. Rosen, eds. *Apartheid: Calibrations of Color.* Icarus World Issues Series. New York: Rosen, 1991.

Naidoo, B. *No Turning Back: A Novel of South Africa.* New York: HaperCollins Juvenile Books, 1999.

Stein, R.C. *Cape Town.* Cities of the World. Danbury, CT: Children's Press, 1999.

Some Websites About South Africa
www.gov.za/yearbook/1998/index.html
www.southafrica.net
www.africa.com

Index

Acknowledgments

Cover Photo Credits
Corbis: Lindsay Hebberd (baskets); Nik Wheeler (Zulu woman making drink) **Image Bank:** S. Achemar (thorn tree); **Brown Partworks Ltd** (accordion)

Photo Credits
AKG London: 52, 55, 61; Ghandi Photo Service 63; **Bridgeman Art Library:** Bonhams London 100; South African Library, Cape Town 56; Stapleton Collection UK 59; **Bruce Coleman:** HPH Photography 27, 32; **Corbis:** Anthony Bannister: Gallo Images 99; Contemporary African Art Collection 71; Michael and Patricia Fogden 6; Hein von Horsten; Gallo Images 50; Charles O'Rear 36, 42; Philip Richardson 86; Franck Seguin: TempSport 112; Peter Turnley 48, 73, 74; Warwick Tarboton: Gallo Images 31; Nik Wheeler 96, 102, 114; **Robert Hunt Library:** 65; **Hutchison Library:** 104; Robert Aberman 93, 118; N. Durrell McKena 111; Aymon Frank 85; Ingrid Hudson 43, 108; M. Kahn 44, 106, 116; **Image Bank:** S. Achernar 98; **Popperfoto:** 67, Peter Andrews; Reuter 76; **Tony Stone Images:** Theo Allofs 39, 80, Chad Ehlers 24; Michelle and Tom Grimm 12; Rainer Grosskopf 79; Frank Herholdt 25; Rolf Hicker 23; Simeone Huber 19; Lewis Kemper 29; Paul Kenward 82; Bob Krist 90; John Lamb 16, 21; Mark Petersen 30; Tom Sheppard 46; Bob Thomas 40; Art Wolfe 34.